THE BEST IN TENT CAMPING:

COLORADO

*A Guide for Campers Who Hate RVs, Concrete Slabs, and
Loud Portable Stereos*

Second Edition

THE BEST IN TENT CAMPING:

C O L O R A D O

*A Guide for Campers Who Hate RVs, Concrete Slabs, and
Loud Portable Stereos*

Second Edition

Johnny Molloy

Menasha
Ridge
Press, Inc.

Library of Congress Cataloging-in-Publication Data

Molloy, Johnny, 1961–
    The best in tent camping, Colorado: a guide for car campers who hate
RVs, concrete slabs, and loud portable stereos/ Johnny Molloy.—2nd ed.
      p. cm.
    Includes biographical references and index.
    ISBN 0-89732-377-7
    1. Camping—Colorado—Guidebooks.   2.Camp sites, facilities, etc.—
Colorado—Guidebooks.   3. Colorado—Guidebooks.   I. Title.
GV191.42.C6M65   2001
647.9788'89'025—dc21

                                                          2001018011
                                                               CIP

Cover Design by Grant Tatum
Cover Photo by Dennis Coello
Maps by Bryan Steven Jones

Menasha Ridge Press
P.O. Box 43673
Birmingham, AL 35243
www.menasharidge.com

CONTENTS

Gold Park 77
Kite Lake 80
Lost Lake 83
Lost Park 86
Mirror Lake 89
Mueller State Park 92
Ruby Mountain 95
Supply Basin 98
Weir & Johnson 101
Weston Pass 104

Southwest Colorado
Alvarado 108
Bear Lake 111
Burro Bridge 114
Cathedral 117
Great Sand Dunes 120
Lost Trail 123
Mesa Verde 126
Mix Lake 129
North Crestone 132
Ridgway State Park 135
Rio Blanco 138
Silver Jack 141
Stone Cellar 144
Transfer Park 147
Trujillo Meadows 150

The Prairie
Bonny Lake 154
Jackson Lake 157

Appendices
Appendix A—Camping Equipment Checklist 163
Appendix B—Information 165
Appendix C—Suggested Reading and Reference 167
Index 169

M A P   L E G E N D

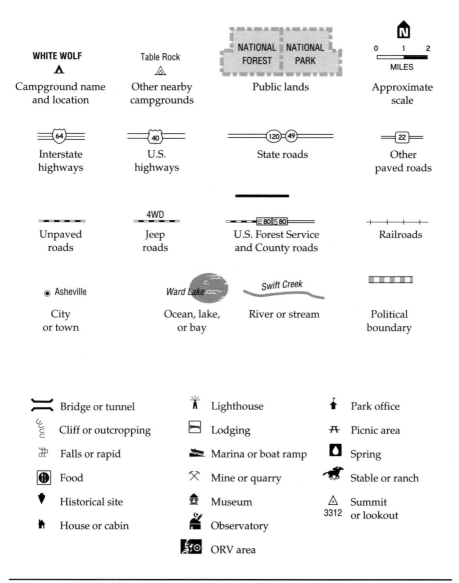

WHITE WOLF
Campground name
and location

Table Rock
Other nearby
campgrounds

NATIONAL FOREST NATIONAL PARK
Public lands

N
0   1   2
MILES
Approximate
scale

64
Interstate
highways

40
U.S.
highways

120 49
State roads

22
Other
paved roads

Unpaved
roads

4WD
Jeep
roads

80 80
U.S. Forest Service
and County roads

Railroads

⊙ Asheville
City
or town

Ward Lake
Ocean, lake,
or bay

Swift Creek
River or stream

Political
boundary

Bridge or tunnel

Cliff or outcropping

Falls or rapid

Food

Historical site

House or cabin

Lighthouse

Lodging

Marina or boat ramp

Mine or quarry

Museum

Observatory

ORV area

Park office

Picnic area

Spring

Stable or ranch

△
3312
Summit
or lookout

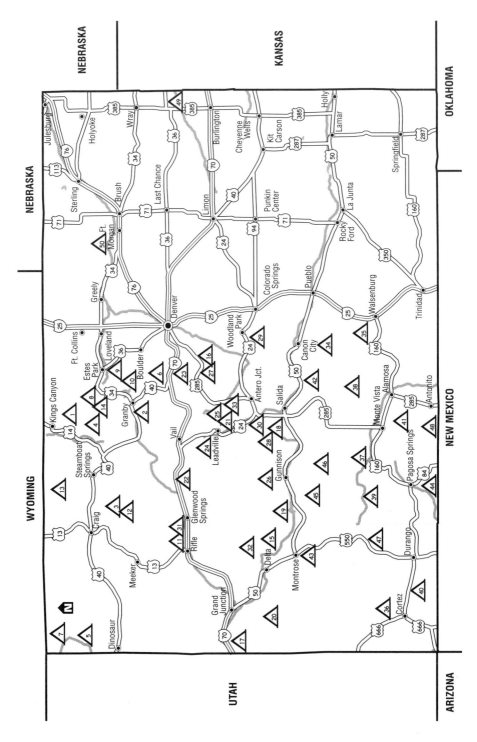

NORTHWEST COLORADO
1. Browns Park
2. Byers Creek
3. Cold Springs
4. The Crags
5. Dinosaur National Monument
6. Golden Gate Canyon State Park
7. Irish Canyon
8. Jacks Gulch
9. Longs Peak
10. Rainbow Lakes
11. Rifle Falls State Park
12. Shepherds Rim
13. Steamboat Lake State Park
14. Timber Creek

CENTRAL COLORADO
15. Black Canyon of the Gunnison National Monument
16. Buffalo
17. Colorado National Monument
18. Cottonwood Lake
19. Curecanti
20. Dominguez Canyon
21. Elbert Creek
22. Fulford Cave
23. Geneva Park
24. Gold Park
25. Kite Lake
26. Lost Lake
27. Lost Park
28. Mirror Lake
29. Mueller State Park
30. Ruby Mountain
31. Supply Basin
32. Weir & Johnson
33. Weston Pass

SOUTHWEST COLORADO
34. Alvarado
35. Bear Lake
36. Burro Bridge
37. Cathedral
38. Great Sand Dunes
39. Lost Trail
40. Mesa Verde
41. Mix Lake
42. North Crestone
43. Ridgway
44. Rio Blanco
45. Silver Jack
46. Stone Cellar
47. Transfer Park
48. Trujillo Meadows

THE PRAIRIE
49. Bonny Lake
50. Jackson Lake

This book is for John Bland. He got it all started.

ACKNOWLEDGMENTS

I would like to thank the following people for their help in getting this book completed: Joe Mayer, Sam Berry, Becky Anderson, Kate Brannan, Paul Welschinger, Susan Webster, Margaret Albrecht, Bryan Delay, James Herbaugh, Pat Molloy, Bill Armstrong, Keith Stinnett, Bryan Hatfield, Michael and Nan Wolfenbarger, Nelle Molloy, Larry of Castle Rock; Beverly, Wilbert, and Craig Spieker of Castle Rock who made me feel at home; Regi Roberts, John Cox, and David Zaczyk, master of the semicolon.

PREFACE

O h, what a joy it was to research this book! In the beginning, the task of finding the 50 best campgrounds in Colorado seemed daunting, for there are hundreds of campgrounds located among the millions of acres of national and state forest land, national parks and monuments, and other public lands. But the months of exploring Colorado's varied landscape turned into a journey through a scenic wonderland. The Rockies come to mind first, where craggy, snow-covered mountains tower over verdant meadows, cool alpine lakes reflect deep forests and cobalt skies, and snow-fed mountain streams crash down narrow valleys. But there are other sides of Colorado: the amazing cliff dwellings of Mesa Verde, the chasm of the Black Canyon of the Gunnison, the alluring reservoirs of the plains, the immense Great Sand Dunes backed against the Sangre de Cristo Range, the whitewater of the Arkansas River, the red rock country of the Uncompahgre Plateau, and more.

After seeing this tremendous variation, I wanted the reader to be able to combine enjoying these sights and with having a quality camping experience at a good campground. I toured the state's natural and historic features by day, then typed up on-site reports from the nearby camps where I stayed, using a computer powered by my car battery.

Each day's experience left me looking forward to the next day, to see if I could find campgrounds to match the beauty of the landscape. Spells of cold and rain and wrong turns and long drives to campgrounds that failed to make the book could not overwhelm the sense of awe I felt while surveying the real Colorado. The subject material overwhelmed the actual physical process of finding the best campgrounds. In other words, researching Colorado was a blast!

And it can be for you, too, pitching your tent at 3,500 feet in the plains or 12,000 feet in the mountains, and just about every elevation and situation in between. Here, you can relax in attractive settings. Beyond the campgrounds you can hike canyons, climb "fourteeners," raft wild rivers, fish remote trout streams, mountain bike tabletop mesas, boat reservoirs, go caving, and recall Colorado's history. Combine this book and a slice of your precious time then do a little exploring of your own.

-Johnny Molloy

THE BEST IN TENT CAMPING:

COLORADO

A Guide for Campers Who Hate RVs, Concrete Slabs, and Loud Portable Stereos

Second Edition

INTRODUCTION

A Word about this Book and Colorado Camping

The Colorado landscape is rich with opportunities for tent camping. Millions of acres of public lands are dotted with hundreds of campgrounds—but you probably only have a precious amount of limited time. Which campgrounds do you choose? Where should you go? When should you go? That's what this book is for—to help you make the wisest use of your time in the wilds of the Centennial State.

In the mountains of Colorado, the Rockies, camping is primarily a summertime activity. When the snow melts and the rivers run high-that's when tent campers start longing for the crisp mornings, crystal clear days, and cool nights by the campfire that are part of a Rocky Mountain camp out. Not to mention wilderness hiking, trout fishing, mountain biking, and whitewater boating.

In other parts of Colorado, the tent camping season is extended. You can pitch your tent year-round in the canyon country of the Western Slope, along the prairie lakes of the east, and in some of the lower elevation state parks. No matter where you go or when you go, the scenic beauty of Colorado will never fail to please the eye.

Before embarking on a trip, take some time to prepare. Many of the best tent campgrounds are at the far end of a gravel road. This isolation—part of their attraction for many campers—makes for a long supply or gear run if you are unprepared. Call ahead and ask for a park map, brochure, or other information to help you plan your trip. Make reservations wherever applicable, especially at popular state parks. Ask questions. Ask more questions. The more questions you ask, the fewer surprises you'll get. There are other times, however, when you'll grab your gear and this book, hop in the car, and just wing it. This can be an adventure in its own right.

The rating system

Included in this book is a rating system for Colorado's 50 best campgrounds. Certain campground attributes—beauty, site privacy, site spaciousness, quiet, security, and cleanliness/upkeep—are ranked using a star system. Five stars are ideal, and one is acceptable. This system will help you find the campground that has the attributes you desire.

Beauty

In the best campgrounds, the fluid shapes and elements of nature—flora, water, land, and sky—have melded to create locales that seem to have been made for tent camping. The best sites are so attractive you may be tempted not to leave your outdoor home. A little site work is all right to make the scenic area camper-friendly, but too many reminders of civilization eliminated many a campground from inclusion this book.

Site privacy

A little understory goes a long way in making you feel comfortable once you've picked your site for the night. There is a trend of planting natural borders between campsites if the borders don't exist already. With some trees or brush to define the sites, everyone has their personal space. Then you can go about the pleasures of tent camping without keeping up with the Joneses at the next site over—or them with you.

Site spaciousness

This attribute can be very important depending on how much of a gearhead you are and the size of your group. Campers with family-style tents need a large, flat spot on which to pitch their tent and still get to the ice chest to prepare foods, all the while not getting burned near the fire ring. Gearheads need adequate space to show off all their stuff to neighbors strolling by. I just want enough room to keep my bedroom, den, and kitchen separate.

Quiet

The music of the mountains—singing birds, rushing streams, wind-blown meadows, and quaking aspen trees—includes the kinds of noises tent campers associate with being in Colorado. In concert, they camouflage the sounds you don't want to hear—autos coming and going, loud neighbors, and so on.

Security

Campground security is relative. A remote campground with no civilization nearby is relatively safe, but don't tempt potential thieves by leaving your valuables out for all to see. Use common sense, and go with your instinct. Campground hosts are wonderful to have around, and state parks with locked gates are ideal for security. Get to know your neighbors and develop a buddy system to watch each other's belongings when possible.

Cleanliness/upkeep
I'm a stickler for this one. Nothing will sabotage a scenic campground like trash. Most of the campgrounds in this guidebook are clean. More rustic campgrounds—my favorites—usually receive less maintenance. Busy weekends and holidays will show their effects; however, don't let a little litter spoil your good time. Help clean up, and think of it as doing your part for Colorado's natural environment.

Helpful hints
To make the most of your tent camping trip, call ahead whenever possible. If going to a state or national park, call for an informative brochure before you set out; this way you can familiarize yourself with the area. The Forest Service website (www.fs.fed.us) allows visitors to view information on each National Forest. The site provides access to the virtual visitors center of each forest, where prosective visitors can obtain campsite information, including notice of closed campgrounds. Also helpful is the Colorado State Parks page (www. parks.state.co.us).

Once you have arrived, ask questions. Most stewards of the land are proud of their piece of terra firma and are honored you came for a visit. They're happy to help you have the best time possible.

If traveling to a national forest, call ahead and order a map of the forest you plan to enter. Not only will this make it that much easier to reach your destination, but nearby hikes, scenic drives, waterfalls, and landmarks will be easier to find. More and more national forests are establishing visitor centers in addition to ranger stations. Call or visit and ask questions. When ordering maps, ask for any additional literature about the area in which you are interested.

In writing this book I had the pleasure of meeting many friendly, helpful people: local residents who were proud of their Colorado landscape, state park and national forest employees who endured my endless barrage of questions, and many campers who shared a cup of coffee and a piece of their time. They already know what a lovely place Colorado is. As the splendor of the Centennial State becomes more recognized, these lands become that much more precious. Enjoy them, protect them, and use them wisely.

NORTHWEST COLORADO

BROWNS PARK

Fort Collins

The lower Laramie River valley has a big country–lonesome feel to it. There aren't too many folks around here, mainly just ranchers. Browns Park is tucked away in some woods on a side creek that feeds into the Laramie. If you want to get away from the people that are trying to get away from it all, come here. This pretty little campground is adjacent to the woods and lakes of the Rawah Wilderness, which covers a stretch of the Medicine Bow Mountains. You can hike and fish here, or just take it easy. Browns Park is great for relaxation. Summer afternoons are as slow as molasses.

After passing the busy campgrounds of the Poudre Canyon and overcrowded Chambers Lake, you'll feel grateful for the peace and quiet here in the Laramie Valley. After entering the campground, notice the facelift it has received from the Forest Service and a little additional alteration by forest beavers—the busy critters built themselves a dam on Jinks Creek and flooded one of the camping loops. A picnic table now lies in a pool of water.

A couple of sites lie in the lodgepole and aspen woods to your right, then the main campground drive splits off to the right and you enter the outer loop. (There used to be one more split off to the right, but the beavers took care of that.) The outer loop turns away from Jinks Creek and runs alongside a slight slope.

CAMPGROUND RATINGS

Beauty:	★★★★
Site privacy:	★★★
Site spaciousness:	★★★★
Quiet:	★★★★
Security:	★★★
Cleanliness/upkeep:	★★★

Browns Park abuts the old-growth forests and alpine lakes of the Rawah Wilderness near the Wyoming border.

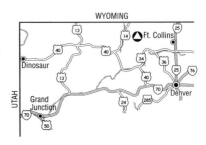

NORTHWEST

The campsites on the outside of the loop are higher than the road, but have been graded and host tent pads for a level night of rest. The inner loop campsites lie in a mixed woods with a very grassy understory augmented by small conifers. Move away from the hill and pass the inner loop. These campsites are more open, but all of the campsites are spread far apart, so privacy can be had by every camper. The inner loop splits Browns Park in half, but the roads are spread far enough apart

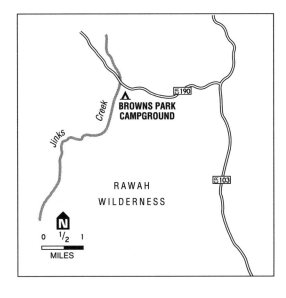

that you won't be bothered by your fellow campers when they drive past. The county road leading in to Browns Park gets less traffic than some campgrounds I've seen.

Complete your loop back to the campground entrance and the new vault toilets. Browns Park has no water—I recommend bringing it with you.

This site has low usage. I met a man on my visit who had been coming to Browns Park for 10 years and had only seen the campground full once. He and his wife were the only campers there on the day I met him. Weekdays can be desolate, which is great for those who love solitude. Summer weekends can be half to two-thirds full, except when the campground fills up for major holidays.

For a nearby natural experience, check out the beaver pond and see if you find any of nature's architects plotting to flood the rest of the campground. Two hiking trails leave from the trailhead adjacent to Browns Park into the Rawah Wilderness, which is far enough from the metropolitan areas to receive little use also.

The McIntyre Trail traces McIntyre Creek to Houseman Park, then turns left to another meadow where beavers have again been busy flooding the trail. These upper beaver ponds offer excellent trout fishing. The Link Trail climbs through a lodgepole forest to a former burned area, where views of the Laramie River valley stretch into Wyoming. You can also see the Poudre Canyon below.

If you want to access the high lakes of the Medicine Bows, take the Rawah Trail, which starts in the Laramie River valley south of Browns Park (you pass this trailhead on the way in). The Rawah Trail crosses several different environments. Leave the valley grasslands, wind your way from lodgepole to spruce fir forest to tundra above the tree line, where there are many bodies of water collectively dubbed the Rawah Lakes.

No matter what you do, bring some friends with you to Browns Park and the Medicine Bows because there might not be too many other people out here, especially during the week. Also, bring all the supplies you may need because the nearest store is not really near at all, though there is a guest ranch nearby down Larimer County Road 103.

To get there: From Fort Collins drive north on U.S. 287 for 11 miles to CO 14. Turn left on CO 14 and follow it for 49 miles west to CR 103 (Laramie River Road). Turn right on CR 103 and follow it for 15 miles. At a T-intersection turn left on CR 80C and travel approximately 3 miles to Browns Park campground.

KEY INFORMATION

Browns Park Campground
Canyon Lakes Ranger District
1311 South College Avenue
Fort Collins, CO 80524

Operated by: Rocky Mountain Recreation

Information: (970) 498-2770; www.fs.fed.us/r2/arnf

Open: June through October

Individual sites: 28

Each site has: Tent pad, picnic table, fire grate, stand-up grill

Site assignment: First come, first served; no reservation

Registration: Self-registration on site

Facilities: Vault toilet (no water)

Parking: At campsites only

Fee: $9 per night

Elevation: 8,400 feet

Restrictions

Pets—On leash only

Fires—In fire grates only

Alcoholic beverages—At campsites only

Vehicles—30 feet

Other—14-day stay limit

BYERS CREEK

Fraser

Grand County prides itself as the mountain biking capital of Colorado. And maybe it is. Over 600 miles of single track, old logging roads, and fire roads are ready for avid pedalers. The Fraser Valley gently slopes up to the rugged Rockies, allowing for varied slopes to suit a bicycler's varied desires. Many of the trails have been improved to attract mountain bikers. Some nearby ski resorts offer lifts, making rides a little faster. Not only bikers, but hikers and fishermen also need a good tent-camping locale. This beautiful valley, rimmed by granite peaks and Byers Creek, is it.

The campground lies in the St. Louis Valley between the Byers Peak Wilderness and the Vasquez Peak Wilderness. At the head of the valley is St. Louis Peak; the Fraser Valley is below. The air cools a bit while driving into the Fraser Experimental Forest where Byers Creek Campground is located. Turn into the campground and note the density of the woods here. Lodgepoles are crowded together with spruce and other conifers, especially along the creek. The thick understory indicates less use than most campgrounds.

Also note the cleanliness of the campground and its overall well-kept appearance. Byers Creek is operated jointly by the U.S. Forest Service and a local Lions Club—and a good job is done by all. The first campsite is on your left just before the small loop begins. The next few campsites

CAMPGROUND RATINGS

Beauty: ★★★★
Site privacy: ★★★
Site spaciousness: ★★★★
Quiet: ★★★★
Security: ★★★
Cleanliness/upkeep: ★★★★

Byers Creek is mountain biking headquarters for the Fraser Valley. There are also two wilderness areas nearby.

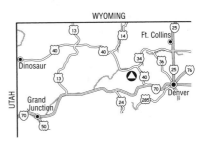

NORTHWEST

on the loop are down from the road in a flat along St. Louis Creek. These sites are for water lovers. Byers Creek flows in upstream and across from the road.

As the road curves left, the only broken stretch of forest is in a flood plain to your right.

A few more campsites sit on a rise away from Byers Creek, but the sites themselves have been leveled. The water and restrooms are in the center of the loop. This is one pretty, intimate campground. But its small

size means fewer sites, and that means the possibility of it being full when you arrive. You needn't worry during the week. It usually will fill on weekends because it is not difficult to fill a six-site campground. (An alternative is the St. Louis Creek campground three miles northeast of Byers Creek. It is not the best in tent camping, but it will do in a pinch.)

Before you drive up to Byers Creek, stop in the Fraser Visitor Center. It is located near the first turn toward the campground. It has some excellent information about biking in the area, including a full-color mountain bike trail map of Winter Park and the Fraser Valley. The map shows miles of trails and rates them by difficulty. There is even a bike trail leaving from the Visitor Center itself!

The trails include forest roads that you can take right from the campground. The west side of Grand County has lesser-used trails. The majority of trails are on public land, so you can concentrate on pedaling instead of worrying whether you are trespassing. Anyway, local folks embrace mountain bikers.

From June through September, mountain biking events are held here, including races and festivals.

The Fraser Valley is not only about mountain biking, however. It is also about hiking and fishing. Half of the 8,095-acre Byers Peak Wilderness is tundra. Wilder-ness areas do not allow bikes, but you can hike the trail to the top of Byers Peak. The trailhead is three miles from the campground, and then it's a three-mile round trip to the top of the 12,804-foot mountain. Much of the nearby Vasquez Peak Wilderness is above the tree line, too. Forest roads splinter off St. Louis Road, offering hikes into the high country of both wildernesses.

At the head of St. Louis Road is the three-mile trail to St. Louis Lake. You can also reach St. Louis Peak from here. Anglers can fish the 11,500-foot St. Louis Lake. There are eight miles of fishing on St. Louis Creek as well. I've only touched on a few of the many outdoor opportunities here.

Make Byers Creek your tent-camping headquarters for the Fraser Valley, then proceed with your favorite activity.

KEY INFORMATION

Byers Creek Campground
Sulphur Ranger District
9 Ten Mile Drive, P.O. Box 10
Granby, CO 80446-0010

Operated by: U.S. Forest Service

Information: (970) 887-4100; www.fs.fed.us/r2/arnf

Open: Memorial Day through Labor Day

Individual sites: 6

Each site has: Picnic table, fire ring

Site assignment: First come, first served; no reservation

Registration: Self-registration on site

Facilities: Hand pump well, vault toilets

Parking: At campsites only

Fee: $10 per night

Elevation: 9,360 feet

Restrictions

Pets—On leash only

Fires—In fire grates only

Alcoholic beverages—At campsites only

Vehicles—32 feet

Other—14-day stay limit

To get there: From Fraser, head west on CR 72 (Elk Creek Road). Follow CR 72 for 0.4 mile to Fraser Parkway (a dirt road). Turn right on Fraser Parkway and follow it for 0.7 mile to CR 73 (St. Louis Creek Road). Turn left on CR 73 and follow it for 7 miles to Byers Creek Campground, which will be on your left.

COLD SPRINGS

Yampa

Do you like camping near a bubbling cascade? Do you like camping near a mountain pond? Do you like camping by a spectacular mountain view? Would you like to enjoy all three of these features and also be next to Colorado's second-largest protected wilderness? Relish all of the above at Cold Springs Campground.

Now, this place isn't perfect, but Cold Springs is an earthly delight. Here, you can leave your tent, fish and hike all day, then return to your little scenic mountain heaven.

All right, let's get to the bad part. It is a little closer to the road than is truly ideal. The campsites could stand to be a little more level. The campground as a whole is pretty broken in, but other than that, it's great.

Turn into the short campground drive and pass the first campsite on your left, in an open meadow with the best of alpine views. Snow-covered Flat Top Mountain lies across the Bear River, which rushes from Stillwater Reservoir above. Behind you, tree-covered slopes rise to mountain lakes. There is a good view down the valley of Bear River as well.

Cross over a small stream, then enter the small loop road. To your right is the mountain pond. Above it, on the hill, are two other streams noisily dropping over rocks into the pond. The second campsite lies in an open meadow next to the pond and the first stream. This is the largest and most popular campsite. The third campsite is

CAMPGROUND RATINGS

Beauty:	★★★★
Site privacy:	★★
Site spaciousness:	★★★
Quiet:	★★★
Security:	★★★
Cleanliness/upkeep:	★★★★

Cold Springs is both the grandstand and springboard for enjoying the eastern Flat Tops Wilderness.

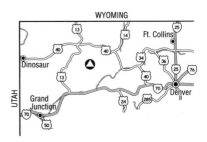

NORTHWEST

close to the pond as well. It offers all views, but no shade.

The fourth campsite is closest to the cascades and has some shade-providing spruce. The fifth campsite is set off in a forested corner of the campground beside a stream of its own. This is the shadiest and most private campsite. An outhouse lies in the center of the loop and a water spigot is close to all campers in this small campground.

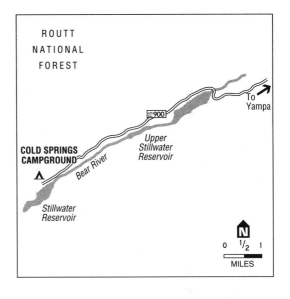

If Cold Springs is full—with only five sites it may very well be on summer weekends—try Horseshoe Campground just a little ways back down Bear River Road. It is has seven campsites and is more forested than Cold Springs; consequently it doesn't have the inspiring views. Cold Springs offers car-free access to the recreational opportunities of the Bear River corridor.

The Flat Tops Wilderness is all around you: cliffs towering over alpine tundra and subalpine terrain, where spruce–fir forests give way to over 110 fish-filled lakes and ponds. Another 100 miles of streams flow through this angler's fantasy land. Just a five-minute jaunt up the road from Cold Springs is a major trailhead, Stillwater, leading into the Flat Tops.

To survey your kingdom for a day, take the North Derby Trail, #1122. Cross the Stillwater Dam to a large park, then climb into the wooded highlands through a burned area, coming to an 11,200-foot pass after about two miles.

Turn left at the pass, leaving the maintained trail, and stay on the divide, rising to the peak of Flat Top Mountain at mile 4. There is a rock pile at the 12,354-foot summit. Look down and see if you can see your friends or spot your tent back at the campsite. You can also stay on the maintained trail and come to Hooper and Keepner Lakes at 3 miles. These are great fishing lakes.

The Bear River Trail, #1120, leaves Stillwater Reservoir west into the wilderness. Pass Mosquito Lake at mile 1.5, a scenic, yet dubious, destination, then climb toward the high country. Once up high, you can go along the Flat Tops in either direction or drop down toward Trappers Lake. The high-country trails are fairly level, for scenic, mild hiking.

The East Fork Trail, #1119, splits off the Bear River Trail and heads north into some superb vistas. Pass Little Causeway Lake at mile 1.2, then climb up toward the Devils Causeway, a side destination from the East Fork Trail. This is a narrow stretch (4 feet wide) of the Flat Top plateau that drops 1,500 feet in either direction. On the main trail you will come to many small lakes and, finally, Causeway Lake at 5 miles. Anglers, be sure to bring your rods.

For those who want hike-free fishing, there are three reservoirs for fishing in the Bear River Corridor. The closest is Stillwater; Yampa and Yamcola reservoirs are downstream. In between these reservoirs flows the Bear River. Fishermen can be seen bank-fishing the lakes and walking the meadows of Bear River. All these waters are stocked.

Limited supplies can be bought back down in Yampa. When you come to Cold Springs, expect to be busy—the great view at the campground will inspire you to be a part of the scenery.

KEY INFORMATION

Cold Springs Campground
Yampa Ranger Disrict
P.O. Box 7, 300 Roselawn Avenue
Yampa, CO 80483

Operated by: U.S. Forest Service

Information: (970) 638-4516; www.fs.fed.us.r2/mbr

Open: Early June through mid-October

Individual sites: 5

Each site has: Picnic table, fire grate

Site assignment: First come, first served; no reservation

Registration: Self-registration on site

Facilities: Water spigot, vault toilets, trash collection

Parking: At campsites only

Fee: $10 per night, $5 in off season (without water)

Elevation: 10,200 feet

Restrictions

Pets—On leash only

Fires—In fire grates only

Alcoholic beverages—At campsites only

Vehicles—22 feet

Other—14-day stay limit

To get there: From Yampa, drive southwest on CR 7 for 17 miles as it turns into FS 900. Cold Springs will be on your right.

THE CRAGS

Gould

The Crags is an appropriate name for this campground. It is balanced on the steep slopes of the Never Summer Mountains. The treeless, granite precipices are not far above you and your vista of Diamond Peaks. The actual Nokhu Crags are behind you and out of sight from the campground. The camping season is short, and nights are always cool here. So reserve a piece of your valuable time in July or August and see what the Colorado State Forest has to offer.

This forest actually abuts Rocky Mountain National Park, so that ought to give you an idea of the level of scenery here. North Park, the vast expanse of meadowland in Jackson County, is known as the moose capital of Colorado. Plan to see a few of those large critters and a few more animals if you explore the trails of Colorado State Forest.

After you drive that dizzying last mile to The Crags, take a deep breath and enter the campground. The setting is a high-country forest of subalpine fir and Englemann spruce growing densely on steep slopes. Fear not, for the campsites have been leveled, though you may have to go up or down a bit to reach the camp from your car.

Don't drive too fast through the loop or you'll miss some of the campsites, which are set back in the woods. A few sites have pull-through areas for your vehicle, but don't expect to see any big rigs up here.

CAMPGROUND RATINGS

Beauty:	★★★
Site privacy:	★★★★
Site spaciousness:	★★★
Quiet:	★★★★
Security:	★★★
Cleanliness/upkeep:	★★★

Colorado State Forest is rich in wildlife and is one of the state's best places to see moose.

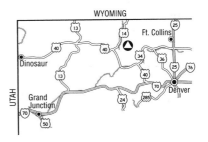

NORTHWEST

That road discourages them, but any passenger car smaller than a moving truck can make the drive.

Enter a sunny area where you will see tree stumps left over from the days when this area was logged. Campsites here have a clear view of the severe lands above them. The loop reenters the woods and the more heavily wooded campsites begin. The last three campsites are very isolated and offer the most solitude. Back at the beginning of the loop are vault toilets for each gender; the hand-pump well is to your left in the woods a bit. The water here is very cold.

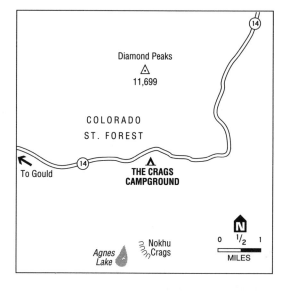

Weekdays rarely find the camp filled. However, on later summer weekends, the campground will be alive with families and young couples, along with a few from the older generation who haven't converted to the dreaded RV. This hidden jewel of a park is not nearly as busy as other Front Range parks.

The Crags is close to some of the 71,000-acre Colorado State Forest's best hiking. Just up the road is the trail to Lake Agnes. It is less than a mile from the trailhead to the lake, which is banked against the Nokhu Crags. A path makes a loop around the lake. American Lakes are accessible by a 5-mile hike and offer views of the Medicine Bow Mountains. Make the one-way walk to Cameron Pass and have a shuttle car pick you up. Watchable wildlife includes mountain lions, elk, mule deer, coyote, and bear.

Ruby Jewel Lake is only a 1.5-mile trek. Kelly Lake and Clear Lake are other destination hikes in the park. If you fish these waters, remember that only artificial lures and flies are allowed. State regulations apply in park streams and in North Michigan Reservoir and Ranger Lakes.

Check out the Visitor Center with the unique barbed-wire moose outside and the stuffed moose inside. There are also informative displays on the park's wildlife that kids will really love.

In 1995, the Colorado Senate declared North Park moose capital of Colorado. Moose were introduced into North Park in the late 1970s and have been thriving here ever since. Try to observe moose in the early morning and late evening in the willow thickets along area creeks. You should also take the auto tour of the Arapaho National Wildlife Refuge in the heart of North Park. Get directions at the Visitor Center.

To get there: From Gould, drive north on CO 14 for 7 miles to FS 170. There will be a sign for Lake Agnes. Turn right on FS 170 and follow it for 0.5 mile to the first intersection. Turn right on FS 172 and climb steeply for 1 mile, turning left at the next intersection. Continue to the Crags Campground.

KEY INFORMATION

The Crags Campground
Colorado Sate Forest
2746 Jackson County Road 41
Walden, CO 80480

Operated by: Colorado State Parks

Information: (970) 723-8366; parks.state.co.us/state_forest

Open: July through September

Individual sites: 26

Each site has: Picnic table, fire grate, tent pad

Site assignment: By advance reservation or pick an available site on arrival

Registration: By phone (call (800) 678-CAMP, (309) 470-1144 in metro Denver), online (www.reserveamerica.com), Visitor Center, or at park entrance

Facilities: Hand-pump well, vault toilets

Parking: At campsites only

Fee: $4 Parks Pass plus $10 per night

Elevation: 10,000 feet

Restrictions

Pets—On leash only

Fires—In fire grates only

Alcoholic beverages—3.2% beer only

Vehicles—No trailers or motor homes allowed

Other—14-day stay limit in 45-day period

DINOSAUR NATIONAL MONUMENT

Dinosaur

The drive down Sand Canyon into Echo Park will amaze you. The scenery at Echo Park will stun you. Rough going on the roads is both a blessing and a curse. The thick dust keeps out a lot of campers, but this is one place where you will never, ever, see an RV, unless its driver is demented.

Echo Park lies just below the confluence of the Green and Yampa Rivers. Colorful vertical canyon walls rise from across the river. The grassy meadow of Echo Park leads to another tan, gray, green, and black cliff face enclosing the park. Across the river is the stone sentinel of Steamboat Rock. A dense ribbon of box elder and cottonwood divides much of Echo Park from the river. The opening of Pool Creek Canyon narrows in the distance. More canyon walls and wooded mountains are downriver. The park continues upriver until the Yampa splits off to the right. Words can't begin to match the true magnificence of Echo Park.

The campground is off to the left, between the river and the meadow as you enter Echo Park. The first campsite is riverside, all by itself; the river access and fee/information booth are past it. Next is a string of four campsites that look over the park from beneath dense, box elder trees. Small paths cut to the river from some of these campsites.

The dirt road continues, then more campsites appear on the riverbank. The picnic tables are lower than the parking spot for

CAMPGROUND RATINGS

Beauty: ★★★★★
Site privacy: ★★★★
Site spaciousness: ★★★★
Quiet: ★★★★★
Security: ★★★★★
Cleanliness/upkeep: ★★★★

This is one of the best tent campgrounds in the entire national park system, but you might want an all-wheel-drive vehicle.

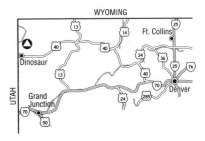

NORTHWEST

these sites. Farther down, the riparian woods break, allowing the next campsites to have views of the Green River and the sheer walls of the canyon beyond. An auto turnaround spot also serves as the parking area for the five walk-in tent campsites that extend upriver.

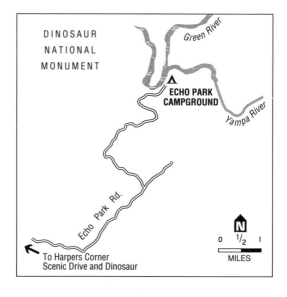

The first walk-in site sits alone beneath an old cotton-wood. The others are a 150-yard walk to a grove of cot-tonwood and box elder trees that are not as dense as the vehicle campsites. A water spigot and vault toilet serve these campsites. Other facilities are conveniently situated for all to use, even though the campground is strung over several hundred yards of the river.

You can count on getting a campsite during summer weekdays, but get to Echo Park early on summer weekends. Campsites are nearly always open during spring and fall. However, always call ahead to see if Echo Park is open, as rains can render the road impassable and close the campground.

On your way down Echo Park Road, enjoy the scenery of Sand and Pool canyons, then stop at the Chew Ranch. This site was not developed until the 1900s. The ranch was occupied as late as 1970, when the owner passed on. Other, more primitive ranch sites are also viewable. Next, you will come to a very interesting Indian petroglyph that was scratched high into the Sand Canyon wall. Whispering Cave is farther down. Walk close to it and feel the refreshing, cool air on a hot summer day.

The Green River will lure you to its banks, but the swift current can make swimming hazardous. Fishing is negligible for channel catfish, which inhabit the stained waters. The photographic opportunities are numerous. You may also want to bring your camera on some day hikes that leave Echo Park.

The Sand Canyon Route heads up the Green River, then veers right up the Yampa to the first canyon on your right. You can follow the trail for miles up to Yampa Bench Road, but I recommend backtracking—it's less dusty than walking on the road. A good late-afternoon hike is the Mitten Park Route. It follows the Green River downstream, high above the left bank. Hike 1.5 miles to another grassy meadow, Mitten Park. It's another good place to look over Steamboat Rock.

Pats Draw is a quickie, canyon-sampler hike. Head back up the road out of the park and veer right just past the second creek ford. This is a short, but easy, there-and-back walk. You can also start back at the Chew Ranch, then follow the Pool Creek Route up the flow of Pool Creek, though the water course can dry up. It intersects Echo Park Road after 3 miles.

Dinosaur National Monument offers much outside of Echo Park. About 27 miles west of Dinosaur, Colorado, in the state of Utah, is the actual museum that is overlaid on the fossilized bones of the dinosaurs that made this place a park. Harpers Corner Scenic Drive offers a worthy auto tour. Some awe-inspiring views are at the end of day hikes that spur off the scenic drive. Commercial outfitters offer rafting opportunities into the deep canyons of the monument as well. It is impossible to resist telling your friends about this place.

To get there: From Dinosaur, head east on U.S. 40 for 1.5 miles to the entrance for Dinosaur National Monument. Turn left on Harpers Corner Scenic Drive and follow it for 23 miles to Echo Park Road. Follow Echo Park Road for 8 dusty miles, then veer left at the signed turn for Echo Park. Follow this road for 5 miles to Echo Park Campground.

KEY INFORMATION

Dinosaur National Monument, Echo Park Campground
4545 East Highway 40
Dinosaur, CO 81610-9724

Operated by: National Park Service

Information: (970) 374-3000 or (435) 789-2115; www.nps.gov/dino

Open: May through September

Individual sites: 17

Each site has: Picnic table

Site assignment: First come, first served; no reservation

Registration: Self-registration on site

Facilities: Water spigot, vault toilet

Parking: At campsites only

Fee: $6 per night

Elevation: 5,000 feet

Restrictions

Pets—On leash only

Fires—No wood fires allowed, only charcoal fires in fire pans

Alcoholic beverages—At campsites only

Vehicles—No RVs or trailers; all-wheel-drive vehicles recommended

Other—14-day stay limit

GOLDEN GATE CANYON STATE PARK

Golden

Golden Gate is a preserved slice of the Rocky Mountains just a few minutes away from Denver. Rock spires stand out among rich forests and green meadows. Vistas offer outstanding views of the Continental Divide to the west. Well-marked and well-maintained trails meander down watery glens to open meadows, where settlements once stood. This refuge is rich in wildlife, from birds to bears. With 55 walk-in tent sites, your camping experience promises to be a good one.

There are two primary campgrounds at Golden Gate Canyon. Reverends Ridge is the big one; it offers spaces for every type of camper. There are ten camp loops of every shape and description, including small circles with parking areas radiating like spokes. There are two loops with pull-through sites for RVs. The old group campground has been converted to six mini-loops that can only be described as different.

But tent campers need only concern themselves with loops F, G, and J in Reverends Ridge; these offer walk-in tent sites. Loops F and G are next to each other. It is a short walk from the parking area to your tent site beneath the lodgepole pines or an aspen or two. Loop J is at the very end of the main camping drive, cutting down on drive-by traffic. Some of the campsites are close to the parking area; others are set back in the woods. A stay at Reverends Ridge offers tent campers a

CAMPGROUND RATINGS

Beauty: ★★★
Site privacy: ★★★
Site spaciousness: ★★★
Quiet: ★★★
Security: ★★★★★
Cleanliness/upkeep: ★★★★

Golden Gate is your quick tent-camping getaway from the Denver metropolitan area.

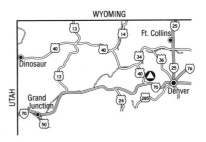

NORTHWEST

compromise: You can stay at the tent sites and still access the water spigots and the hot showers and flush toilets located in the camper services building.

Aspen Meadow, on the other hand, is more rustic and is the preferred area for tent campers. It has hand-pump wells and vault toilets. But it is also more scenic and isolated from the rest of the campground. Aspen Meadow itself is broken up into three distinctive walk-in tent camping areas.

Tremont
Mtn.

GOLDEN
GATE
STATE

▲ GOLDEN GATE CANYON   PARK
CAMPGROUND

Golden Gate Canyon Rd.

To Golden

N

0   ¹/₂   1

MILES

The Meadow Loop has 14 campsites in a conifer and aspen wood, next to a large meadow. The campsites on one side of the dirt road are situated amid large boulders that add to the character of the area. The Twin Creek and Conifer loops are off the ridge in a small valley. The woods are more dense here, and a small stream adds to the setting. These are the most popular tent-only sites and are the first to be claimed. Some of the campsites are nearly 100 yards away from the parking area.

The Rimrock Loop has several wooded campsites up on a ridge punctuated with boulder landscaping; these sites offer a view of the lands in the distance. These campsites also have the pump well nearest to them. Vault toilets are set in each loop at Aspen Meadow.

No matter where you camp, reservations are highly recommended and practically mandatory for summer weekends. Go ahead and make the call to ensure yourself a preferred campsite. Weekdays are not such a problem in this safe, family-oriented campground and natural area.

While you are in the campground, check the notices about ranger programs that are held nightly on weekends. You can learn about the human and natural history of the park in these talks led by park naturalists. There are kids' programs on weekend days that cater specifically to young campers who want to have a good time and learn something about nature without feeling like they are in school.

Other campers will want to strike out on their own on some of the 35 miles of park trails. Everyone should walk the Raccoon Trail. It begins at Panorama Point, where you have a fantastic view of the Continental Divide, and it has interpretive signs to teach hikers a thing or two. The most popular loop hike is the Mountain Lion Trail, which winds for 7 miles into Forgotten Valley, back up a canyon, and up by Windy Peak. Take the side trail to the top of Windy Peak.

Also, the walk into Frazer Meadow is one of the more picturesque park settings. There are three ways to get to the meadow, including the Mule Deer Trail, which connects to Aspen Meadows Campground. There are five ponds in the park and a few small streams that offer trout fishing. Dude's Fishing Hole is very near Aspen Meadows. Denverites should take advantage of this quick getaway to the real, natural Colorado.

To get there: From Golden, take CO 93 north for 1 mile to Golden Gate Canyon Road. Turn left and follow Golden Gate Canyon Road for 15 miles to the park.

KEY INFORMATION

Golden Gate Canyon State Park Campground
3873 Highway 46
Golden, CO 80403

Operated by: Colorado State Parks

Information: (303) 582-3707 or (303) 642-3856 in the summer; parks.state.co.us/golden_gate

Open: Aspen Meadow Loop: year-round; Reverends Ridge Loop: May through October

Individual sites: 55 walk-in tent sites, 86 other

Each site has: Picnic table, fire grate, tent pad

Site assignment: By advance reservation or on site

Registration: By phone (call (800) 678-CAMP or (303) 470-1144 in Denver)

Facilities: Hot showers, flush and vault toilets, laundry, phone, vending machines; 28 sites have electricity

Parking: At campsites or walk-in tent campers parking area

Fee: $4 Parks Pass plus $10 per night walk-in tent site at Aspen Meadows; $10 per night walk-in tent sites Reverends Ridge; $14 per night for electrical hookups

Elevation: 9,100 feet

Restrictions

Pets—On leash only

Fires—In fire grates only

Alcoholic beverages—3.2% beer only

Vehicles—40 feet

Other—14-day stay limit in 45-day period

IRISH CANYON

Maybell

Irish Canyon is for adventurous tent campers. It is off the beaten path and then some in the extreme northwest corner of the state on Bureau of Land Management (BLM) land. This is in the Browns Park area, where Butch Cassidy and his gang retreated to safety between heists at the turn of the century. Irish Canyon itself is named for a trio of robbers who lit down the gorge after a hold-up in nearby Rock Springs, Wyoming.

These days you can enjoy the scenery and solitude of Irish Canyon, then venture out to a host of sights including Indian petroglyphs, Vermillion Falls, Lodore Hall, Browns Park National Wildlife Refuge, the Gates of Lodore, and more.

Irish Canyon is only 100 yards wide as you enter it. High rock walls drop down to sage, grass, and boulder fields. Gnarled old pinion and juniper trees rise along the wall in places. When you come to the campground, the sage gives way to old trees that climb up Cold Spring Mountain. Across the canyon is a sharp, high wall of rock, where small trees cling to precipices. I arrived at Irish Canyon in the afternoon, when the sun burned into the wall so brightly it shone. Later, a full moon rose over the canyon, making it easy to imagine outlaws tending stolen cattle rustled into the gorge.

A teardrop loop enters the forest of old junipers and pinion, above a campsite that overlooks the quiet road traversing the canyon. This site has two tables for larger

CAMPGROUND RATINGS

Beauty: ★★★★★
Site privacy: ★★★
Site spaciousness: ★★★
Quiet: ★★★★
Security: ★★
Cleanliness/upkeep: ★★★

If you really want to get away from it all, come here. You'll see a whole different side of Colorado.

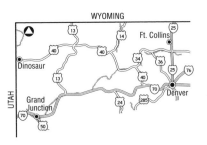

24

NORTHWEST

groups. The second site also overlooks the flat below and the immense wall, but has ample shade.

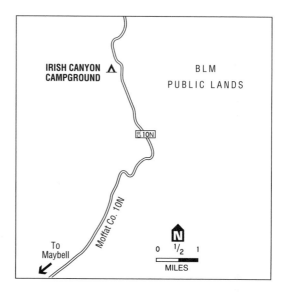

The campsites farther up the loop are more secluded. The campsite atop the loop is large and is the most private. Three more campsites occupy somewhat leveled areas on the way back down. The picnic table pads have all been leveled, but some tent sites have a slight slope to them. A single vault toilet lies in the wooded interior of the loop for all to use. No water is provided; you must bring your own. Browns Store, 10 miles from the camp and west down State Road 318, has water, gas, a phone, and limited supplies. They also rent out canoes if you want to float down a quiet section of the Green River.

This is a very isolated camp; still, it has a road along it. So if you worry about leaving your gear unattended, have your adventures, then set up camp and stay there. This area no longer hosts robbers; most passers-by are friendly local ranchers, so you needn't be concerned about theft. Nor should you be concerned with Irish Canyon filling up. Campsites are available year-round.

At a place like Irish Canyon, you have to explore and make your own adventures. There are no rangers to tell you what to do or handouts laying everything out. It is wise to contact the BLM office in Craig for information to help you plan exactly what you want to do.

On your way from Maybell, watch for signs leading to local sights and make note of their particular roads. The old coke ovens are near Greystone. The Sand Wash Basin has a herd of wild horses. On the way in, stop at Vermillion Falls. It's a pretty, yet strange, sight: a cascade in such dry land. You can also explore

Vermillion Creek and its colorful, badlands canyon by foot or mountain bike on old jeep roads. The Gates of Lodore is the entrance to a magnificent canyon, where the Green River leaves Browns Park and crashes downstream to meet the Yampa River at Dinosaur National Monument. A trail leaves the picnic area at the entrance of the canyon to see some Indian petroglyphs, possibly inscribed by two different tribes on the same rock.

The hiking and mountain biking around Irish Canyon is limited only by your stamina. Marked trails are few, but jeep roads are many. Below the canyon, paths lead up Green Canyon onto Peek-a-boo Ridge and a sweeping view of Browns Park below. Old jeep roads lead up Talamantes Creek farther up the canyon onto Cold Spring Mountain. Unless on foot, stay on the roads.

Drive down to Browns Park National Wildlife Refuge to absorb a little human and natural history. Thousands of birds stop here during spring and fall migration. Elk and deer make this ribbon of green their home during the winter. You can make the 11-mile auto tour of the refuge and see the old Lodore Hall, where you'll find another petroglyph rock and the Two Bar Ranch. This was the stomping ground of Butch Cassidy. Thanks to the proximity of three states, Colorado, Utah, and Wyoming, ruffians could slip across state lines and out of jurisdiction when lawmen chased them.

I loved this area; finding it was a steal, better than the loot Butch Cassidy and the Wild Bunch were after.

To get there: From Maybell, drive west on U.S. 40 for 0.5 mile, then turn right on CO 318 and follow it for 41 miles to CR 10N. Turn right on CR10N and follow it 8 miles to Irish Canyon Campground, which will be on your left.

KEY INFORMATION

Irish Canyon Campground
Little Snake BLM Field Office
455 Emerson Street
Craig, CO 81625

Operated by: Bureau of Land Management

Information: (970) 826-5087 or (970) 826-5000; www.co.blm. gov/lsra/lsraindex.htm

Open: Year-round

Individual sites: 6

Each site has: Picnic table, steel fire ring

Site assignment: First come, first served; no reservation

Registration: No registration

Facilities: Vault toilet (bring water)

Parking: At campsites only

Fee: No fee

Elevation: 6,650 feet

Restrictions

Pets—On leash only

Fires—In fire rings only

Alcoholic beverages—At campsites only

Vehicles—30 feet, on roads only

Other—14-day stay limit

JACKS GULCH

Fort Collins

Jacks Gulch is a model campground in many respects. It has separate camping areas for separate types of campers, including RV, horse, and tent campers. No one intrudes on each other's space and a good time is had by all. One thing the Forest Service could not improve on is the natural setting for Jacks Gulch. It is simply beautiful: a huge flat with mixed forest of ponderosa pine and aspen, interspersed with flower-laden meadows. Many of the tent sites are on the edge of a lovely meadow. The Forest Service did, however, tastefully integrate the campground into this attractive environment.

Enter Jacks Gulch Campground on the main road. Off to your right is the Equestrian Camp. There are five sites with the same amenities as the regular campsites, except they each have a minicorral for the horses. The sites are large and spread farther apart than the average campsites. The two group campgrounds are also over this way.

Veer left, then stay straight and come to the Yarrow Loop. Nice campsites with the newest grills, grates, tent pads, and picnic tables add to the naturally appealing setting. All manner of campers can enjoy this loop, where most of the campsites are shaded by large ponderosa pines.

The other loop is the Columbine Loop; it weaves around like a snake. The campsites have electrical hookups in addition to the

CAMPGROUND RATINGS

Beauty:	★★★★★
Site privacy:	★★★★
Site spaciousness:	★★★★
Quiet:	★★★★
Security:	★★★★
Cleanliness/upkeep:	★★★★

Jacks Gulch is the forest campground of the future. It has a little bit of something for everyone, including ten attractive walk-in tent sites.

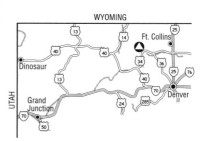

NORTHWEST

standard amenities. This is
the home of the big rigs.
Splintering off this loop,
however, is the walk-in tent
campers area. There is a
water spigot and vault toilet
in the parking area for tent
campers to use. Follow a little gravel path away from
the parking area into an
aspen wood mixed with
some conifers. The camp-
sites themselves splinter off
from the main gravel path
on a gravel path of their
own. Each campsite is far
from its neighbor. It's almost
like each site is its own
miniature campground. I highly recommend this tent-camping experience.

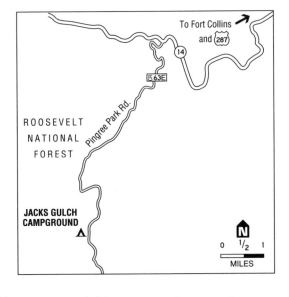

The first five sites have a path of their own, and the second five campsites
have their own path as well. Each of these paths connects to the gravel
Campground Loop Trail, which makes for a good morning leg-stretcher.

Up Flowers Road beyond the campground is the Flowers Trail. You may
have to walk part of the four-wheel-drive road to get to it. After intersecting
Beaver Park, enter the Comanche Peaks Wilderness. Elk roam this wilderness,
which is also known for its fishing. Leave Beaver Park and climb up to
Browns Lake. This path was an old wagon trail in the 1800s.

Little Beaver Creek Trail and Fish Creek Trail enter the wilderness just a little south of the campground on County Road 44H. Both make moderate
ascents up their respective watersheds and offer trout fishing for hikers and
horseback riders. Other trails enter the wilderness from forest roads south of
Jacks Gulch. Consult your Arapaho and Roosevelt National Forest map,
which you should buy before coming to Jacks Gulch. Not too far south is the
northern border of Rocky Mountain National Park, which can be accessed by

foot from Pingree Park up the Mummy Pass Trail.

You can also make Jacks Gulch a base camp for recreating in the Poudre Canyon. Rafters, kayakers, and fishermen all will be seen in and around the river, testing the waters. This campground is much more desirable than those in the canyon, yet it is only 6 miles from the canyon and river. You can leave the crowded canyon with its roadside campgrounds and return to Jacks Gulch, where the scene is much quieter and the camping is some of the best in the state.

To get there: From Fort Collins, drive 10 miles north on U.S. 287 to CO 14. Turn left on CO 14 and follow it for 24 miles to CR 63E (Pingree Park Road). You will see a sign for Pingree Park. Turn left on CR 63E and follow it for 6 miles to Jacks Gulch Campground, which will be on your right.

KEY INFORMATION

Jacks Gulch Campground
Canyon Lakes Ranger District
1311 South College Avenue
Fort Collins, CO 80524

Operated by: Rocky Mountain Recreation

Information: (970) 498-2770; www.fs.fed.us/arnf

Open: May through October

Individual sites: 10 walk-in tent only, 5 equestrian, 55 other

Each site has: Picnic table, fire grate, stand-up grill, tent pad

Site assignment: First come, first served; no reservations

Registration: Register with camp host

Facilities: Water spigots, vault toilets, some sites have electricity

Parking: At campsites and walk-in tent parking area

Fee: $13 per night

Elevation: 8,100 feet

Restrictions

Pets—On leash only

Fires—In fire grates only

Alcoholic beverages—At campsites only

Vehicles—50 feet

Other—14-day stay limit

LONGS PEAK

Estes Park

Longs Peak Campground offers the best and worst of the American national park system. This tents-only camping area is located in a scenic setting adjacent to some of the most beautiful mountain land in the Rockies. There are many sights to see and things to do, but the very things that attract you to this park also attract many other visitors.

Longs Peak is an extremely popular hike here. Cars will line the road leading to the trailhead and campground. It takes a combination of timing and luck to get a campsite during the peak season, which is from late June through mid-September. When you do get a campsite, you will realize that in spite of all the cars nearby, the hustle and bustle won't overwhelm you in this 26-site campground. The trailhead parking area, however, will have all the hustle and bustle.

Pass the line of parked cars along Longs Peak Road and come to a split in the road. Turn right and enter the campground. To your left is the always-full-during-the-summer trailhead parking. The teardrop-shaped, gravel campground loop makes its way beneath a lodgepole woodland pocked with boulders and smaller trees. The campsites are mostly on the outside of the loop and have somewhat obstructed views of the Twin Sisters peaks across the Tahosa Valley in the Roosevelt National Forest.

More campsites are stretched along the peak side of the loop. As popular as they

CAMPGROUND RATINGS

Beauty: ★★★
Site privacy: ★★
Site spaciousness: ★★★
Quiet: ★★
Security: ★★★★
Cleanliness/upkeep: ★★★★

This tent-only campground can be your base camp for exploring the east side of Rocky Mountain National Park.

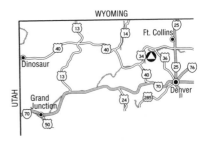

NORTHWEST

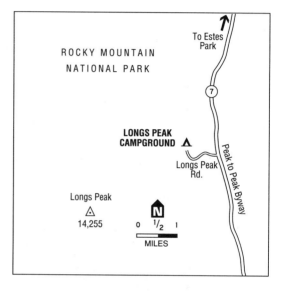

are, they are well maintained. A hill rises against the campground. This is the campground' rockier side; campsites are more spread out over here. Overall, the sites are average in size, with ample room for the average tent. But always being full does make the place seem a bit confined. Colorful tents and colorful people give Longs Peak some extra pizzazz.

Water spigots are situated around the campground, but there is only one toilet for each gender located in the center of the campground. You might have to wait in line for that, too. Realistically, you will feel lucky and appreciative when you do get a campsite; you'll still have a pleasurable tent camping experience here. Try to get here on the shoulder seasons—June or late September—and you can get a campsite much easier. Bring your own water and a warm sleeping bag if you come in winter.

I recommend auto-touring the park your first day, maybe doing some shorter hikes, then tackling Longs Peak first thing the next morning, when you have all day to make the climb. Driving Trail Ridge Road is a must. It is a rite of passage at Rocky Mountain National Park. The views are as exhilarating as the air is cold up there. Then check out the exhibits and self-guiding nature trail at Moraine Park Museum. Back at Longs Peak, take a warm-up hike on the Storm Pass Trail. It leads up to the Eugenia Mine Site and onto Storm Pass after 2.5 miles.

Then go to bed early. Your route to the top of Longs Peak will be the Keyhole Route, which is generally free of snow from mid-July until mid-September. The final part of the route is 1.6 miles beyond the end of the maintained trail; most of the scramble is marked on the rock below you.

The park service recommends that you try to leave the trailhead between 3 a.m. and 6 a.m. to make the 7.5 miles to the summit of Longs Peak by noon. Bad weather can arise at any time, but it is more likely in the afternoon during the summer. Bring plenty of warm clothes and plenty of lung power. The round trip lasts from 12 to 15 hours. Make sure and keep your campsite a second night because you will be too exhausted to do anything except make supper and hit the sack.

Just a few miles south of Longs Peak is the Wild Basin area, a quieter section of the park's east side. Many old-time Rocky Mountain enthusiasts consider this to be the best area of the park. There are many watery features in the basin that make great day hikes. It is only 0.3 mile from the Ranger Station in Wild Basin to Copeland Falls. Calypso Cascades is 1.8 miles up where St. Vrain Creek splits. Ouzel Falls is 2.7 miles up the trail from the Ranger Station. Continue a little farther to see the peaks above and the plains below. There are several alpine lakes to access in Wild Basin.

KEY INFORMATION

Longs Peak Campground
Rocky Mountain National Park
Estes Park, CO 80517

Operated by: National Park Service

Information: (970) 586-1206; www.nps.gov/romo

Open: Year-round

Individual sites: 26

Each site has: Picnic table, fire grate, tent pad

Site assignment: First come, first served; no reservation

Registration: Self-registration on site

Facilities: Water spigot, flush toilets (no water October through May)

Parking: At campsites only

Fee: $16 per night (Memorial Day through mid-September) or $10 in the off season plus $7 one-week auto pass

Elevation: 9,400 feet

Restrictions

Pets—On leash only

Fires—In fire grates only

Alcoholic beverages—At campsites only

Vehicles—Tents only, no RVs

Other— 7 nights per campsite

To get there: From Estes Park, head south on CO 7 for 8 miles to Longs Peak Road. Turn right on Longs Peak Road and follow it for 3 miles to Longs Peak Campground, which will be on your right.

RAINBOW LAKES

Nederland

The last couple of miles to Rainbow Lakes are bone-jarringly bumpy. But once here you'll wonder why you haven't come sooner. It is an old campground that has received a makeover. The picnic tables, grates, and grills are new; however, the Forest Service did cap the water well, so now you must bring your own water.

The campground is just south of Rocky Mountain National Park and is adjacent to the equally scenic Indian Peaks Wilderness. The forest here is upper-level montane, primarily lodgepole, with some Englemann spruce and a few aspens struggling to survive. On my late June visit, the aspens had barely started leafing out. Their short growth time coincides with the short time this campground is open.

If you are in the area, stay here. The Rainbow Lakes are only half a mile from the campground. Make your visit up to the lakes for the day, and camp down at the campground. That preserves the natural resource and concentrates your impact at the campground. Rainbow Lakes Campground can also be a base camp for exploring the east side of Rocky Mountain National Park. Be forewarned: This campground receives heavy weekend use in the late summer.

Rainbow Lakes Campground lies along a stream emanating from the Rainbow Lakes that feed into Caribou Creek. Willows and beaver ponds break up the meadow to

CAMPGROUND RATINGS

Beauty: ★★★★
Site privacy: ★★★
Site spaciousness: ★★★★
Quiet: ★★★★
Security: ★★★
Cleanliness/upkeep: ★★★

Rainbow Lakes is Boulder County's best high-country tent camping getaway.

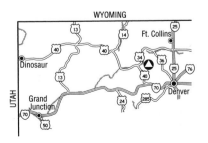

NORTHWEST

your left; on your right is a rising woodland. The first three sites are on a spur to your right. One is a pull-through site, but don't expect to find RVers up here unless they enjoy tearing up their rig. Continue up the main drive and another loop spurs off your right. It contains six campsites that are beneath conifers. The two sites inside the spur loop are a little small.

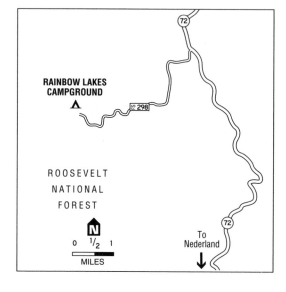

RAINBOW LAKES
CAMPGROUND

ROOSEVELT
NATIONAL
FOREST

0   ½   1

MILES

To
Nederland

The rest of the campsites border the stream and are spread apart well beneath the trees. The last campsite is away from the others, next to the trailhead parking area for Rainbow Lakes. Three vault toilets for this small campground are overkill, but at least you won't have to walk far to the bathroom no matter where you are camped.

Stated simply, come here during the week or Sunday night if at all possible. Not only is the campground full on weekends but there is also significant traffic coming through the campground to and from the Rainbow Lakes trailhead. Vacationers should stay here during the week and tour the national park.

From Nederland you drove part of the Peak to Peak Scenic Byway. Continue to enjoy this drive north to Estes Park, where there are supplies, and south to Black Hawk, where there is legalized gambling. The casinos offer limited stakes gaming.

However, a sure bet is the Indian Peaks Wilderness next door. The glaciers in the Indian Peaks are the southernmost ones in North America. This high wilderness starts at 10,700 feet. Much of the scenery is the austere tundra, rock, and ice. The Rainbow Lakes Trail goes the half a mile to the lakes; it is a must-hike.

The Arapaho Glacier Trail runs in and out of the wilderness a few miles up to the Arapaho Glacier overlook. The glacier is on this side of North Arapaho Peak. It is 6 miles from the trailhead to the Arapaho Pass Trail. Other trailheads into the busy Indian Peaks lie north off forest roads that intersect the Peak to Peak Byway.

Another area to consider is the Wild Basin of Rocky Mountain National Park. This is a watery place, where many cascades tumble down from the heights and picturesque lakes lie beneath craggy peaks. The basin is north on the Peak to Peak Byway. Get hiking information from the Ranger Station there.

For a little bit of interesting civilization, try the college town of Boulder nearby. This eclectic place is known for the wide variety of people who end up here. Take a walk down the Boulder Mall, where the streets are blocked off and freedom reigns supreme. Nearby Nederland, the last stronghold of the 1960s, is a more toned down version of Boulder, where the folks don't work quite so hard at being different. They just are different. Make a visit to Nederland part of your Rainbow Lakes experience.

To get there: From Nederland, drive north on CO 72 for 6.5 miles to FS 298 (also known as CR 116). There will be a sign for University of Colorado Mountain Research Station. Turn left on FS 298 and follow it for 6 miles to Rainbow Lakes Campground.

KEY INFORMATION

Rainbow Lakes Campground
Boulder Ranger District
2140 Yarmouth Avenue
Boulder, CO 80501

Operated by: U.S. Forest Service

Information: (303) 444-6600; www.fs.fed.us/arnf

Open: July through September, sometimes longer

Individual sites: 16

Each site has: Picnic table, tent pad, fire grate, stand-up grill

Site assignment: First come, first served; no reservation

Registration: Self-registration on-site

Facilities: Vault toilets (bring water)

Parking: At campsites only

Fee: $6 per night, plus $3 for a second vehicle

Elevation: 10,000 feet

Restrictions

Pets—On leash only

Fires—In fire grates only

Alcoholic beverages—At campsites only

Vehicles—20-feet

Other—14-day stay limit

RIFLE FALLS STATE PARK

Rifle

Try this one on for size: Colorado's favorite year-round waterfall was created from limestone buildup behind an ancient beaver dam, and these are the cliffs we see today. The falls became a nineteenth-century tourist attraction, then were used as the impetus for Colorado's first hydroelectric plant. The plant was then dismantled and a state park was built around the picturesque site. The state later renovated the park and campground into what we see today. Bet you didn't know beavers could be that constructive.

No matter how the falls came to be—and I am skeptical about that beaver dam story—the falls are here now and you can delight in them and the lakes of Rifle Gap State Park, Harvey Gap State Park, rock climbing at Rifle Mountain Park, the East Fork Rifle State Fish Hatchery, and more outdoor recreation in the White River National Forest nearby. All this can be enjoyed from your base camp at the pleasing walk-in tent sites set in the riparian lushness of the East Fork Rifle Creek.

Park your car at Rifle Falls and take the Squirrel Trail that runs along East Fork Rifle Creek. The campsites spur off the Squirrel Trail. The first campsite is set beneath tall, narrowleaf cottonwoods and is the only site not along the creek. Continue on and you'll find more sites scattered among the box elder, willow, grass, and cottonwoods of the creek bottom.

CAMPGROUND RATINGS

Beauty: ★★★★
Site privacy: ★★★★★
Site spaciousness: ★★★★
Quiet: ★★★
Security: ★★★★★
Cleanliness/upkeep: ★★★★

Rifle Falls is the scenic centerpiece of the Rifle Valley. Set up your base camp here and explore the nearby parks and forest land.

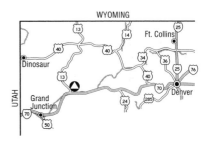

NORTHWEST

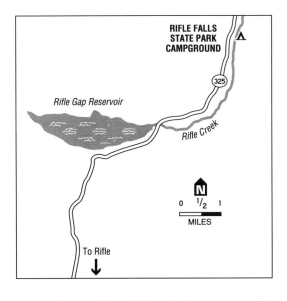

All the sites have been renovated and are more appealing than ever. Each campsite is completely separated from the rest; the farther down the path, the more separated the sites become. The stream sends out a constant symphony of whitewater music. The final campsite is mostly surrounded by the creek, and it is the most isolated and one of the best tent sites in the entire state park system.

Thirteen drive-in sites comprise the balance of the campground, which caters to RVs. These sites have been renovated as well and the whole campground has a tidy appearance to it that meets the high standards of Colorado state parks. Water spigots and new vault toilets have been built to serve the area.

If you want to stay here, get a reservation. There is no reason not to make the five-minute phone call to eliminate the horror of a full campground. Get a reservation no matter when you come. This campground is open year-round.

Of course, Rifle Falls will probably be your first visit. Feel the mist as water plunges down three chutes to the pool below. Take the trail to the top of the falls and see the caves that are there, too. Another hiking opportunity is the Squirrel Trail, which crosses the creek below the falls and explores the waterside lushness of this valley.

Speaking of water, if you vie for trout in the creek and none bite, head a short ways up the valley to the state fish hatchery. They are open for visitation and at least you can take a look at a trout—actually hundreds of them.

Farther up the valley is Rifle Mountain Park. This is where the rock climbers do their work, scaling the sheer walls of the East Fork Rifle Creek canyon.

Even if climbing isn't your thing, check out the free show and admire their bravado. Fishermen take note that the creek is stocked up here. Farther up the creek is the White River National Forest. The Three Forks Trail leaves Three Forks Campground and makes a loop up by Coulter Lake back to the Spruce Picnic Area.

Below Rifle Falls is Rifle Gap State Park. Boaters and jet skiers make wakes through the 350-acre impoundment, and there is a swimming beach for those who like their water sports a little slower. The fishing here can be fast or slow, depending on your skill and luck, of course. Harvey Gap State Park offers more aquatic pleasures and is just a few miles away. There is no waterskiing here; you are more likely to see windsurfers cutting a wake. The 160-acre lake has trout and warmwater fish such as smallmouth bass and crappie.

The city of Rifle is nearby for any supplies you might need, so pitch your tent at the falls and enjoy all there is to enjoy in this little Colorado valley with a big punch.

To get there: From Rifle, drive west on U.S. 6 for 3 miles to CO 325. Turn right on CO 325 and follow it for 10 miles to Rifle Falls State Park, which will be on your right.

KEY INFORMATION

Rifle Falls State Park Campground
00050 Road 219
Rifle, CO 81650

Operated by: Colorado State Parks

Information: (970) 625-1607; parks.state.co.us/rifle_falls

Open: Year-round

Individual sites: 7 walk-in tent sites (Squirrel), 13 drive-in sites (Falls)

Each site has: Walk-in sites have picnic table, fire grate, tent pad; drive-in sites have picnic table, fire grate, electricity

Site assignment: By advance reservation or pick an available site on arrival

Registration: By phone (call (800) 678-CAMP or (303)70-1144 in Denver) or at park entrance

Facilities: Water spigot, vault toilets

Parking: At campsites only

Fee: $4 Parks Pass plus $7 per night tent sites, $14 per night drive-in sites

Elevation: 6,500 feet

Restrictions

Pets—On leash only

Fires—In fire grates only

Alcoholic beverages—3.2% beer only

Vehicles—None

Other—14-day stay limit

SHEPHERDS RIM

Buford

The Trappers Lake area is one of superlative beauty. This beauty is what spawned the wilderness movement as we know it today. In 1919, Forest Service employee Arthur Carhart was surveying the Trappers Lake area in order to lay out a road to and around the lake. He was to plot out some cabin sites on the lake. On seeing the beauty of the forest, water, and cliffs of this high country, he realized this was one place where human works simply couldn't improve on nature. He did complete the survey; however, he let his views be known to his supervisors that some natural places should be set aside in their original state.

This idea of preservation that Carhart started culminated in the Wilderness Act of 1964; today there are over 3 million acres of wilderness land set aside in Colorado alone. The nearest wilderness, the Flat Tops Wilderness, nearly encircles Trappers Lake. There are several campgrounds in the immediate Trappers Lake area, but Shepherds Rim is the best campground for tent campers.

Shepherds Rim is set in a thick spruce forest that is left intact wherever possible, integrating the campground into the woods. A slight slope has required the Forest Service to erect retaining walls and some steps between the road and the actual camping areas to level the campsites, making them more camper-friendly.

CAMPGROUND RATINGS

Beauty:	★★★★
Site privacy:	★★★
Site spaciousness:	★★★
Quiet:	★★★
Security:	★★★★★
Cleanliness/upkeep:	★★★★

This is the best tent campground at Trappers Lake, birthplace of the wilderness movement.

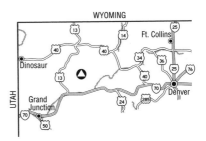

NORTHWEST

With several small camp-sites and parking spots, the layout of Shepherds Rim discourages the bigger rigs from camping here, despite the presence of a few drive-through campsites. In general, the abundance of tent pads means a majority of overnight visitors are tent campers.

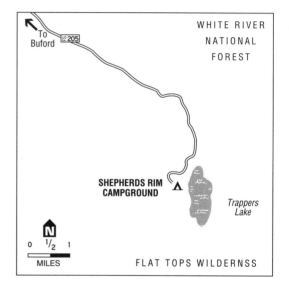

Enter the long and narrow campground loop, then pass the first drive-through camp-site (even though it is drive-through, it also has a tent pad). Most of the campsites are on the outside of the loop, increasing privacy. Short paths connect parking areas to the picnic tables to the tent pads. The tent pads are often farther back in the woods, making for better privacy.

The sites at the back of the loop are the most private. There is a special hand-icapped-accessible site, a double campsite for larger parties, and a camp-ground host to make your stay safe and pleasant. Overall, the Forest Service has upgraded this spot into a well-kept, quality campground that you can use as a base camp to enjoy this area.

Water recreation centers around Trappers Lake, over 300 acres of picturesque Flat Tops splendor. Cliffs rise above the forest and reflect off the clear, clean tarn, where brook and native cutthroat trout thrive. No motors are allowed here, so bring a paddle along with your canoe to enjoy the peaceful environ-ment. Fishing is by artificial flies and lures only. Possession limit is eight for the nearly pure strain of cutthroats. There is no possession limit on brook trout. Other fishing opportunities are along the North Fork of the White River below Trappers Lake and along Fraser Creek, which feeds Trappers Lake.

You can combine hiking and fishing by using many of the trails that radiate from Trappers Lake into the surrounding Flat Tops Wilderness. The nearest trail to Shepherds Rim is the Wall Lake Trail, #1818. It leads up and away steeply from the campgrounds to reach the Flat Tops Plateau after 3 miles. Meadows and forest intermingle here. Wall Lake, 2 miles farther, offers fishing for cutthroat trout.

The Carhart Trail, #1815, roughly circles Trappers Lake in a 4.5-mile loop. It parallels the east and north shore of the lake, allowing for angling opportunities, but pulls away from the lake as it crosses Fraser Creek to intersect the Wall Lake Trail. The Stillwater Lake Trail spurs off the Carhart Trail and heads east to Little Trappers Lake and other fishable lakes. It also offers views of the Chinese Wall, an impressive blockade of rock that extends for miles.

Buy all your supplies before coming to Trappers Lake, then plan to stay a while. This body of water and the surrounding Flat Tops are among the best locations in the state—and that is saying a lot.

KEY INFORMATION

Shepherds Rim Campground
Blanco Ranger District
317 East Market
Meeker, Colorado 81641

Operated by: U.S. Forest Service and Rocky Mountain Recreation

Information: (970) 878-4039; www.wildernet.com

Open: June or July through September

Individual sites: 20

Each site has: Picnic table, fire grate, some tent pads

Site assignment: First come, first served; no reservation

Registration: Self-registration on-site

Facilities: Water spigot, vault toilet

Parking: At campsites only

Fee: $14 per night

Elevation: 9,900 feet

Restrictions

Pets—On leash only

Fires—In fire grates only

Alcoholic beverages—At campsites only

Vehicles—36 feet

Other—10-day stay limit

To get there: From Buford, take CR 8 east for 18 miles (it turns into FS 8) to FS 205. Turn right on FS 205 and follow it for 8 miles to a Trappers Lake Campgrounds sign. Turn right and Shepherds Rim will be 1 mile up on your right.

STEAMBOAT LAKE STATE PARK
Steamboat Springs

Some places get reputations. As I scoured the state in search of the best tent campgrounds, Steamboat Lake kept coming up as an unquestionable inclusion for this book. I was expecting something special, and I wasn't disappointed. It started with the new Visitor Center and ended with the view from the walk-in tent sites from Bridge Island. In between was the town of Steamboat Springs—in my opinion Colorado's most attractive resort—Hahns Peak, Pearl Lake, and the Mount Zirkel Wilderness.

Don't be turned off by the large number of campsites here. They are divided over two major campgrounds. The tent area is set apart on an island and is the main concern to us tent campers.

The Sunrise Vista Campground has 113 sites on the eastern edge of Steamboat Lake. If you are going to stay here, try the Harebell Loop. There will be big rigs here, but this loop nevertheless offers the closest lakeside campsites at Sunrise Vista. The Larkspur Loop is well shaded. The Yarrow Loop also has some lakeside sites, but is dominated by RVs.

The Dutch Hill Campground has 85 campsites. The Wheeler and Baker Loops have electric hookups and are dominated by RVs. Pass the camper services building (with showers, laundry, and so on) near the marina, then arrive at Bridge Island, tent camper's heaven. The first 15 campsites are

CAMPGROUND RATINGS

Beauty: ★★★★
Site privacy: ★★★
Site spaciousness: ★★★★
Quiet: ★★★
Security: ★★★★★
Cleanliness/upkeep: ★★★★

You can enjoy not only all that this state park offers but also thousands of acres of surrounding national forest and the resort town of Steamboat Springs.

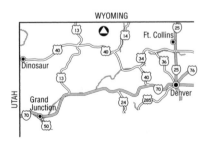

NORTHWEST

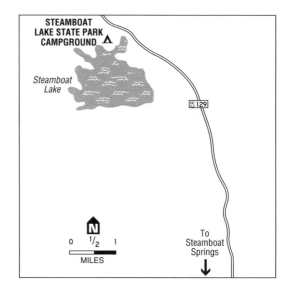

on a loop beneath lodgepole pine. These are drive-up sites that are a little too crowded for my taste. But they are on the island, and the eight campsites on the outside of the loop are near the water.

But the best is last: On the far side of this loop is the parking area for the tent-only campsites. These last 20 sites occupy the part of the island that juts out farthest into Steamboat Lake. The walk to the campsites ranges anywhere from 20 to 200 feet, but the lake and mountain views get better the farther you are from the parking area.

The walk-in campsites are situated in wooded areas between fields that are far from one another. A gravel path spurs off the main gravel loop, connecting the campsites. The sites are dispersed so that campers on the interior of the loop have a quality view as well. The southernmost campsites are the best and most isolated. Boaters can actually pull their craft onto the shore of the island and walk to their campsites.

As the loop swings around, the campsites enter heavy lodgepole woods. The view is across to the marina. These are the least desirable, but still good, walk-in sites. Two vault toilets serve the immediate area, though full facilities are nearby at the camper service building.

If you want to stay here, get a reservation, though the tent sites are the last to be filled. This park has a strong following among the locals, which speaks volumes about its quality. Front Range campers make the drive to overnight here, so do out-of-staters. I repeat, make a reservation to secure a campsite.

Steamboat Lake is, naturally, a park attraction. All manner of water sports are enjoyed on the lake. Skiers, fishers, and personal watercraft enthusiasts use the reservoir. A power zone and a no-wake zone make Steamboat Lake enjoyable for all park visitors. The inlets of the lake offer the best fishing for rainbow, brown, arctic grayling, and native cutthroat trout. If you didn't bring your own watercraft, anything from canoes to pontoon boats can be rented at the park marina, where they also have limited supplies.

Nearby Pearl Lake is another scenic component of the state park system. It offers trout fishing on a smaller reservoir. This is a wakeless lake, so it's a quieter fishing destination.

If you want to get around on foot, first hop in your car and enjoy the Routt National Forest, which nearly encircles Steamboat Lake. Hahns Peak is a popular hike. The Mount Zirkel Wilderness is east of Steamboat Lake. The Slavonia trailhead is your best bet for enjoying this glacier-carved highland, where hundreds of alpine lakes dot the landscape. Take the Slavonia Trail up to Gilpin Lake, then loop back down Gold Creek. The Encampment River and North Fork Elk River offer hiking and angling opportunities. A map is sold in the Routt National Forest Visitor Center, which has over 2,000 square feet of interpretive displays.

For a taste of the city life, visit Steamboat Springs. This resort town has class. Stop at the Visitor Center there and learn about local rodeos, music festivals, and other events. Then you can return to your island campsite at Steamboat Lake.

To get there: From Steamboat Springs, drive west on U.S. 40 for 2 miles to CR 129. Turn right on CR 129 and follow it north for 26 miles to Steamboat Lake State Park.

KEY INFORMATION

Steamboat Lake State Park Campground
Box 750
Clark, CO 80428

Operated by: Colorado State Parks

Information: (970) 879-3922; parks.state.co.us/steamboat

Open: Mid-May through October

Individual sites: 20 walk-in tent only, 198 other

Each site has: Picnic table, fire grate, tent pad; 55 others have electricity also

Site assignment: By advance reservation or pick an available site on arrival

Registration: By phone (call (800) 678-CAMP or (303) 470-1144 in Denver) or at campground booth

Facilities: Hot showers, flush and vault toilets, laundry, phone, vending machines, marina store

Parking: At campsites or walk-in tent campers parking area

Fee: $4 Parks Pass plus $10 per night walk-in tent site, $10 per night nonelectric vehicle sites, $14 per night electric vehicle sites

Elevation: 8,100 feet

Restrictions

Pets—On leash only

Fires—In fire grates only

Alcoholic beverages—3.2% beer only

Vehicles—None

Other—14-day stay limit

TIMBER CREEK

Grand Lake

Timber Creek reminds me of an old-time national park campground: wood smoke curling up through the evergreens; families mingling; couples—both young and old—interacting; tents of every size, shape, and description spread through the campground; and a few pop-up trailers and bigger rigs thrown in for good measure. Everyone is moving at a relaxed, vacation pace. Someone is grilling something tasty, another person is rigging their fishing rod, yet another is snoozing in a lawn chair. You get the feeling that all is well here.

Timber Creek lies in a wooded flat alongside the headwaters of the Colorado River. Trail Ridge Road forms the other boundary. Lodgepole pine is the primary tree here. Pine needles and an occasional rock form the understory. The campsites are spread out in this sizable campground on a main drive with four loops spurring off it. The odd thing is that the loops are named after trees that don't even grow in this park (dogwood is one example)! The main drive passes the Ranger Station and passes some large campsites. Just across from the Ranger Station are the first tent-only campsites. The tent campsites have a car pull-in area, then your campsite is in the woods across planted wood poles separating the camping and parking areas.

The main drive swings alongside the willows of the Colorado River. A few riverside

CAMPGROUND RATINGS

Beauty: ★★★★
Site privacy: ★★★
Site spaciousness: ★★★
Quiet: ★★★
Security: ★★★★★
Cleanliness/upkeep: ★★★★

Timber Creek is your best bet for getting a good tent campsite in Rocky Mountain National Park. Once you are in, there is a lot to see and do.

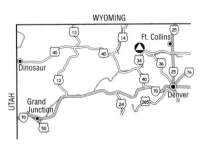

NORTHWEST

sites are in mixed shade and sun and are the best campsites here. The river and mountain view is nice. The rest of the campground is well shaded by lodgepole pine. The first camping loop splits off to the left and has tent-only and general-use sites. The next loop has tent-only and general-use campsites, also. The third loop has only general campsites, but tenters are the majority here, too. The fourth and final loop has mostly tent-only sites.

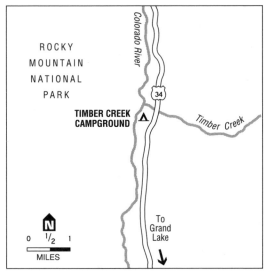

There are several beaver ponds off in the meadow toward the river. Other wildlife, notably moose and elk, have been known to wander through the campground (I saw some elk during my visit here).

Water spigots and comfort stations are spread throughout Rocky Mountain National Park's least busy campground. However, it often fills during the peak season. Timber Creek nears capacity nearly every night from late June to early August. You can generally find a campsite until late in the day Sunday through Thursday. Campsites are usually gone by noon on Friday and Saturday. Finding a campsite in the off-season is no problem, though campground roads are not snowplowed.

If you haven't driven Trail Ridge Road, drive it. It is a rite of passage for first-time park visitors. Campers also like to see the wildlife, fish, and hike the area trails. The Never Summer Ranch Trail leaves from the lower part of the campground. It is a mere half-a-mile walk to this early-era guest ranch. The buildings and grounds have been preserved by the park. Interpretive rangers are on site there in the summer.

The Green Mountain Loop is a popular day hike for Timber Creek campers. It starts down U.S. 34. See Big Meadow and the ruins of a pioneer cabin on this 8-mile tramp. The much shorter River Trail Loop starts down by the Kawuneeche Visitor Center. It runs along the Colorado River and offers views of the Never Summer Mountains above. The path to Timber Lake presents good scenery and is a 10-mile round-trip hike. There are many other trails in the area. The ranger on duty at the campground can steer you on a hike to meet your abilities and desires.

The Colorado River offers fair fishing for brook, brown, rainbow, and cutthroat trout. But serious fishers will head down to the Arapaho National Recreation Area by Grand Lake. The fish are bigger, and the lake is stocked regularly.

Back at the campground, ranger programs are held every night during the summer from mid-June to Labor Day. But mostly campers at Timber Creek will be seen piddling around their campsites. It's called relaxing and having a good time.

To get there: From Grand Lake, head north on U.S. 34 for 10 miles and Timber Creek Campground will be on your left.

KEY INFORMATION

Timber Creek Campground
Rocky Mountain National Park
Estes Park, CO 80517

Operated by: National Park Service

Information: (970) 586-1206; www.nps.gov/romo

Open: Year-round

Individual sites: 33 tent-only sites, 67 other

Each site has: Picnic table, fire grate, tent pad

Site assignment: First come, first served; no reservation

Registration: Self-registration on site

Facilities: Water spigot, flush toilets, phone (no water late September through May)

Parking: At campsites only

Fee: $16 per night, $10 in off season

Elevation: 8,900 feet

Restrictions

Pets—On leash only

Fires—In fire grates only

Alcoholic beverages—At campsites only

Vehicles—38 feet

Other—7-day stay limit per campsite

CENTRAL COLORADO

BLACK CANYON OF THE GUNNISON NATIONAL MONUMENT

Crawford

You won't believe what a deep and narrow gorge the Black Canyon is until you actually see it. There are many places to access the gorge, but the north rim is the best. It is the most quiet and boasts the better campground in the park, set on the rim's edge in an ancient piñon-juniper forest. Instead of looking up at snowy mountains—your typical Colorado view—you will be looking down into a nearly 2,000-foot-deep canyon. Views can be had by hiking or by a scenic drive. You can hike along the rim or drop down into the gorge itself, where the fishing is great along a stretch of Colorado's Gold Medal Waters. The best climbing in the state can be done here at the "Black," as it is known in the climbing world.

Make your drive from Crawford and slightly descend to the canyon along Grizzly Gulch. Turn right, pass the Ranger Station, and come to the North Rim Campground. Enter the loop and the piñon-juniper forest, which is complemented with Gambel oak and the bird-attracting serviceberry. As you look for a campsite, note the gnarled trees here. Some are over 700 years old! It is a rare opportunity indeed to camp among such ancient trees.

The campground lies on a fair slope heading down toward the canyon. The smaller gorge of SOB Draw (which is short for what you think it is) wraps around the campground. Campsites are on both sides

CAMPGROUND RATINGS

Beauty: ★★★★
Site privacy: ★★★
Site spaciousness: ★★★
Quiet: ★★★★
Security: ★★★★★
Cleanliness/upkeep: ★★★★

The North Rim Campground is a rock climber's mecca. However, if you don't climb, come here anyway; there are other ways to enjoy the gorge-ous scenery.

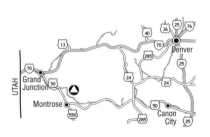

of the road beneath the old trees, which offer the ideal amount of sun and shade. The understory is primarily dirt, which can make for a dusty campsite. Overall, the campsites are on the small side, which discourages nearly all but tent campers, especially after big rig drivers see how the old trees crowd the road. They just turn right around. A vault toilet and water spigot are in the center of the small campground. Be advised that the water may not be turned on early or late in the camping season.

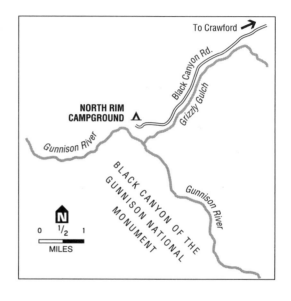

At the end of the loop is the Chasm View Trail. During my visit with a friendly ranger, he raved about this trail. I just had to hike it first thing. Even after the hype, the view into the gorge was simply unbelievable. It is so narrow and deep! The Gunnison River emits its roar, but it is fairly faint up here. There are old trees on the Chasm View Trail, too. It made me want to hit the other views in the park.

The North Vista Trail leaves from the ranger station. The path goes along the north rim of the Gunnison to a high point on a nearby ridge. There are views into SOB Draw. But the highlight is the side trip to Exclamation Point. And as the ranger stated, "They call it Exclamation Point for a reason." Some of the best views of the inner canyon are found here.

So you want to make the challenging descent to, and even more challenging ascent from, the canyon floor? There are three ways in from the North Rim. The SOB Draw Route starts near the campground. It is two hours down and four hours up the 2-mile route. Watch for the poison ivy growing thick along the route. Long Draw is a mile-long drop that starts near the Balanced Rock Overlook; beware of poison ivy growing 5 feet high here. Slide Draw is very steep and starts near the Kneeling Camel View. Fishermen in search of the big trout can brave the poison ivy and test the lesser-fished waters.

There are views along the 5-mile gravel road where you can tour the north rim by car. Simply leave the campground and keep driving along the rim. Be very careful—the views are quite distracting. At the end of this road is the Deadhorse Trail. This 2.5-mile path traces an old road past springs and provides views into Deadhorse Gulch and the main canyon.

The ranger on duty near the campground is often a climbing ranger. The ranger has a route book for climbers to consult and will assist you in choosing routes. Inexperienced climbers should go with other climbers first or stick to the trails. All climbers and backcountry visitors must obtain a free back country permit at the ranger station.

The Black Canyon of the Gunnison is a unique physical feature of Colorado and is a must-see for both natives and tourists.

KEY INFORMATION

North Rim Campground
102 Elk Creek
Gunnison, CO 81230

Operated by: National Park Service

Information: (970) 641-2337; www.nps.gov/blca

Open: Mid-May through mid-October

Individual sites: 13

Each site has: Picnic table, fire grate

Site assignment: First come, first served; no reservation

Registration: Self-registration on site

Facilities: Water spigot, vault toilet

Parking: At campsites only

Fee: $10 per night; $7 park pass per vehicle

Elevation: 7,700 feet

Restrictions

Pets—On leash only

Fires—In fire grates only

Alcoholic beverages—At campsites only

Vehicles—26 feet

Other—14-day stay limit

To get there: From Crawford, drive south on CO 92 for 3 miles to Black Canyon Road. Turn right on Black Canyon Road and follow it as it twists and turns through the countryside for 6 miles to Black Canyon Monument Road. Turn left on Black Canyon Monument Road and follow it for 5 more miles to the monument. Once at the monument, turn right at the first intersection to access the North Rim Campground, just a short distance away.

CENTRAL COLORADO

BUFFALO

Bailey

So many of the best national forest campgrounds are high in the Rockies, where the weather and roads can be rough. Buffalo Campground, at 7,400 feet, is high enough to escape the heat of the lowlands, but not so high that you'll be dressing for winter in July. A network of trails, including the Colorado Trail, winds through the immediate area of ponderosa pine and strange rock formations that burst forth from the needle-carpeted forest floor. This haven in the Pike National Forest is only 70 miles from the metropolitan Denver area.

Buffalo is situated in a stand of mature ponderosa pine on a gentle slope. Flowers, grasses, and juniper ground cover spread over the open, parklike forest floor. An ideal mix of sun and shade makes its way through the evergreen onto the very large campsites. The largest of tents will have no problem setting up on leveled areas at each campsite. But this openness cuts down on camper privacy.

Pass the fee station and begin climbing up the hillside. Pass an inner loop that splits off to your left and has seven campsites that are more open than most because they border a small clearing lying in the center of the main loop. Most of the campsites are on the outside of the main loop and extend far back from the road. The higher you are on the loop, the better you can see a stone outcrop across the way where rock climbers go to work.

CAMPGROUND RATINGS

Beauty: ★★★★
Site privacy: ★★
Site spaciousness: ★★★★★
Quiet: ★★★
Security: ★★★★
Cleanliness/upkeep: ★★★

Buffalo is a quick getaway for metro Denver–area mountain bikers, hikers, and families.

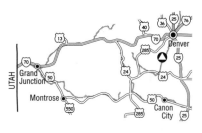

53

A campground host is stationed on the loop to quell any late-night parties or direct you to many of the recreation opportunities in the area. The campground was recently refurbished, and its vault toilets have been replaced. The three water spigots are very reliable.

You can reserve a site here, but Buffalo rarely fills, barring major summer holidays. Weekends usually see a mix of families and youthfull active folks, the vast majority of whom are tent campers. Buffalo is quiet during the week; you can be assured of a campsite.

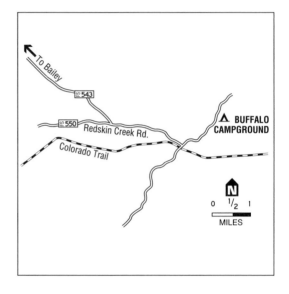

No matter when you come, there is plenty to enjoy in the surrounding Pike National Forest.

As mentioned, rock climbers scale the formation across from the campground. Mountain bikers are seen everywhere, riding the trails that wind through the Buffalo Recreation Area and beyond. A favorite ride is the Colorado Trail. Keep going up the hill from the campground and you will intersect the trail. You can turn left out of the campground on the Colorado Trail and bike to Colorado 126, then return via Forest Service Road 550. Trail #722 makes a loop off the Colorado Trail south. Just off FS 550, there is another loop that heads toward Miller Gulch. Make up your own loop in the trails that twist and turn amid the pines and pillars of stone.

Buffalo Creek, flowing just below the campground, offers trout fishing and more mountain biking along FS 543 that parallels Buffalo Creek. Still more biking trails splinter off FS 543. Wellington Lake, at the upper drainage of Buffalo Creek, is a private lake that offers pay trout fishing and boat rentals.

Hikers can enjoy the same trails as the mountain bikers, but at a slower speed. You can also head into the Lost Creek Wilderness, just a few miles northwest of Buffalo. From the trailhead off Wellington Lake Road, hikers can take the Colorado Trail into the wilderness high country or walk the Craig Meadows Trail into Craig Creek. Other hikes into this wilderness are also accessible from this trailhead.

In the summer there is still enough light to make the drive from Denver or Colorado Springs and be sitting by a campfire at Buffalo at dusk. Cook up a good supper, then retire to the tent. Next morning you can jump out of the tent and onto your favorite trail.

KEY INFORMATION

Buffalo Campground
South Platte Ranger District
19316 Goddard Ranch Court
Morrison, CO 80465

Operated by: U.S. Forest Service

Information: (303) 275-5610; www.fs.fed.us/r2/psicc/spl

Open: Mid-May through Labor Day

Individual sites: 45

Each site has: Picnic table, fire ring, tent pad

Site assignment: By reservation or first come, first served if site available

Registration: By phone (call (877) 444-6777) or self-registration on site

Facilities: Water spigot, vault toilet

Parking: At campsites only

Fee: $11 per night

Elevation: 7,400 feet

Restrictions

Pets—On leash only

Fires—In fire rings only

Alcoholic beverages—At campsites only

Vehicles—22 feet

Other—14-day stay limit

To get there: From U.S. 285 in Bailey, head southeast on CR 68 (it turns into FS 543) for 8 miles to FS 550. Turn left on FS 550 (Redskin Creek Road) and follow it 4 miles to Buffalo (not Buffalo Springs) Campground, which will be on your right.

COLORADO NATIONAL MONUMENT

Fruita

Some folks, when they see something, they just go for it. In 1907, Jim Otto came to the canyon country southwest of Grand Junction and deemed it the most beautiful place he had ever seen. He thought it worthy to be a national park; he single-handedly developed trails among the forests and rock sculptures while simultaneously promoting the land with a few converts from Grand Junction. Four years later, Colorado National Monument was established. Jim's devotion to the park persisted until 1927, when he relinquished his $1-per-month job as park caretaker.

What foresight he had in protecting such a colorful landscape! Now, you can enjoy it, too. Saddlehorn Campground is near many park features and hosts a few features of its own. After climbing out of the valley below, veer left around the Saddlehorn (it really does look like a saddlehorn) and enter the campground. A forest of juniper and piñon emerge from the rust-red soil. Occasional rocks emerge from the fiery dirt among the sage. The whole campground has a slight slope toward the cliffs of the Colorado Plateau, which drop off into the Grand Valley of the Colorado River. Across the valley is the East Tavaputs Plateau and the Grand Mesa. The views are striking.

The campground water spigots are tastefully piped into native stone that add a little extra touch to Saddlehorn. The junipers

CAMPGROUND RATINGS

Beauty: ★★★
Site privacy: ★★★
Site spaciousness: ★★★
Quiet: ★★★★
Security: ★★★★
Cleanliness/upkeep: ★★★★

Deep canyons, red rock, and natural stone sculptures characterize this unique Colorado spectacle.

here are bushy; they pro-
vide decent campsite privacy, but the noonday sun will
beat you down in midsum-
mer. Be forewarned, from
mid-May until early July,
small gnats rule this area
and can drive you buggy.

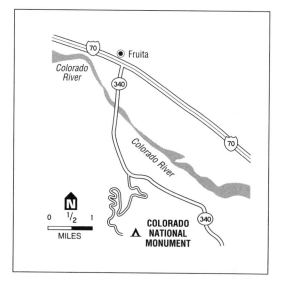

A Loop has 20 sites that
offer great views into the
valley. Several of the sites
are screened from the loop
road. B Loop is very similar
to A Loop and has some
very private sites and great
views. The lights of Grand
Junction shine down below
after dark.

C Loop is part of the original campground built in the 1930s. The campsites
are a little smaller than what we are accustomed to today. It offers views of the
valley and into the monument, but it is only open if the other loops are full,
which normally occurs during Memorial Day weekend only. Otherwise you
can bank on getting a campsite here.

The best time to visit Colorado National Monument, on the advice of a long-
time park ranger, is mid-September to mid-November. The weather has
cooled, the bugs are long gone, and the hiking is great. You can actually walk
from your tent to some of the best day hikes in the park. The Window Rock
Trail makes a short loop and offers photographic views. The Canyon Rim Trail
travels on the edge of Wedding Canyon for more views. And views are what
this monument is all about. Springtime attracts locals for wildflower viewing.

Another ranger recommendation is the Ottos Trail. It drops down toward
the Pipe Organ and overlooks the depths of Monument Canyon. If you are
here during the summer, use the middle of the day to make the 23-mile scenic
drive from one end of the park to the other. There are numerous overlooks—

you will wear your brakes out stopping at all the dramatic canyon scenes. Road bikers also enjoy pedaling the scenic road. The combination of scenery against the backdrop of the plateau and valley country make for one photo op after another!

There are several longer trails that range from 6 to 8 miles. The Monument Canyon Trail enters the heart of the natural rock sculptures. Climbers can be seen scaling Independence Rock. If you are interested in climbing, stop at the park Visitor Center, where they have a book on climbing routes in the monument. Whether you climb or not, remember to be up high at dark—the sunsets and sunrises here are something to see. Rangers hold interpretive programs on summer weekends.

Colorado National Monument is a destination in its own right. But if you are traveling along I-70, don't just glance up and say you've seen this place. The scenery will surprise you while you look down at the folks who thought it wasn't worth their time.

KEY INFORMATION

Colorado National Monument, Saddlehorn Campground Fruita, CO 81521

Operated by: National Park Service

Information: (970) 858-3617; www.nps.gov/colm

Open: A Loop year-round, B Loop April through mid-October, C Loop when necessary; no water in winter

Individual sites: 80

Each site has: Picnic table, stand-up grill

Site assignment: First come, first served; no reservation

Registration: Self-registration on site

Facilities: Water spigots, flush toilets

Parking: At campsites only

Fee: $10 per night

Elevation: 5,800 feet

Restrictions

Pets—On leash only

Fires—No wood fires, charcoal fires in grills only

Alcoholic beverages—At campsites only

Vehicles—None

Other—14-day stay limit

To get there: From I-70 in Fruita, head south on CO 340 for 2 miles to the entrance of Colorado National Monument. Proceed into the monument for 5 miles, and Saddlehorn Campground will be on your left.

COTTONWOOD LAKE

Buena Vista

The Collegiate Peaks are a showy range of mountains that features numerous "fourteeners" (mountains over 14,000 feet elevation). Cottonwood Lake is nestled between Mount Princeton and Mount Yale along South Cottonwood Creek. Hiking amid the wooded and open slopes of these mountains is a popular pastime. However, the stream and lake fishing and an opportunity to unwind are the biggest draws to Cottonwood Lake, where the wily fish may be the ones that give you a schooling.

Come to the campground shortly beyond the attractive Cottonwood Lake. The camping area is perched on a slope just below Sheep Mountain, where you may actually see some mountain goats. The top of Mount Princeton is visible across the valley. Short clusters of aspen grow in the campground, interspersed with small, grassy clearings.

Most of the campsites are spread along a drive that veers up the hill and drops back down to the dirt road that brought you here. A smaller, inner drive splits the main campground in two.

The campsites are spacious and decently separated, but have a broken-in look to them. Since the campground is set on a slope, most campsites offer aspens for privacy, but the aspens are short enough to avail good views of the mountain land across the creek. The lower sites are serenaded by South Cottonwood Creek, if the wind isn't blowing too hard.

CAMPGROUND RATINGS

Beauty:	★★★
Site privacy:	★★★
Site spaciousness:	★★★★
Quiet:	★★
Security:	★★★★
Cleanliness/upkeep:	★★★

Cottonwood Lake offers the best tent camping on the eastern slope of the Collegiate Peaks.

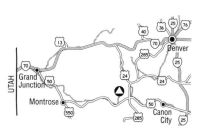

Cottonwood Lake Campground is known for being windy. It is also known to have bears visit every now and then, so store your food in the trunk of your vehicle. Despite these two possible down sides, this campground brings repeat visitors who fill the campground almost daily from July 4 through Labor Day. The weather can be a little iffy in June, so the campground stays about half full. Later in the summer, campers will see afternoon showers, which are normally brief.

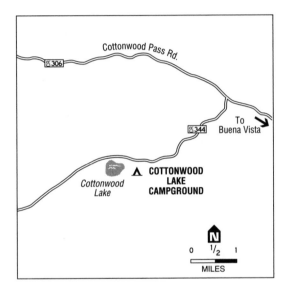

So what brings tent campers back year after year? Cottonwood Lake has a reputation as a good fishery. It is stocked periodically during the summer. Folks fish from the banks and enjoy the scenery, too. Others venture out in small rafts or canoes. Fly fishermen use float tubes to go for trout. Only hand-propelled craft are allowed on Cottonwood Lake. This maintains the pleasant atmosphere. Others fish for brook trout in South Cottonwood Creek, which flows along County Road 344. There are also numerous beaver ponds in which to toss a lure. Farther up the road is the trail to Ptarmigan Lake, off Forest Service Road 344-3A. Fishing is decent in the lake, as well as in a few other small lakes in the vicinity.

If you look across the mountain from the campground, you will see an old road switchbacking up to the high country; follow this to the site of an old silver mine. Look for mountain goats on your way up. A portion of the Colorado Trail crosses the road to Cottonwood Lake. Mountain bikers can go a good distance south, but northbound peddlers will hit the foot-traffic-only Collegiate Peaks Wilderness quickly.

You can climb Mount Yale, which is located in the Collegiate Peaks Wilderness. The trailhead starts on Cottonwood Pass Road, just beyond Collegiate Peaks Campground. You don't need any mountaineering skills to ascend the mountain, just a little staying power. It is 4.5 miles to the top, rising nearly 4,800 feet up Delaney Gulch.

If you want to relax, stay in the campground. But if you want to explore without breaking a sweat, take the drive up to Cottonwood Pass, which is the main road from Buena Vista. The scenic drive is paved all the way to the top of the 12,126-foot break in the mountains. After any activity, you can enjoy the Cottonwood Hot Springs at the bottom of the road. Watch for the sign on your way in to the campground. The springs will be on your right.

KEY INFORMATION

Cottonwood Lake Campground
Grand Valley Ranger District
325 West Rainbow Boulevard
Salida, CO 81201

Operated by: Rocky Mountain Recreation

Information: (970) 242-8211; www.fs.fed.us/r2/psicc/sal

Open: Memorial Day through mid-September

Individual sites: 42

Each site has: Picnic table, fire grate

Site assignment: First come, first served; no reservation

Registration: Self-registration on site

Facilities: Water spigot, vault toilets

Parking: At campsites only

Fee: $10 per night

Elevation: 10,000 feet

Restrictions

Pets—On leash only

Fires—In fire grates only

Alcoholic beverages—At campsites only

Vehicles—30 feet

Other—14-day stay limit

To get there: From Buena Vista, drive 7 miles west on CR 306 (Cottonwood Pass Road) to CR 344. Turn left on CR 344 and follow it four miles to Cottonwood Lake Campground, which will be on your right.

CURECANTI

Gunnison

The best tent campground at Curecanti National Recreation Area is Ponderosa Campground. Ponderosa is ideally located to enjoy all the recreational possibilities not only at Curecanti but also at the West Elk Wilderness just a few miles away. The volcanic rock formations above the waters of Blue Mesa Reservoir and the heavily forested high country of the West Elk contrast with each other. Ponderosa Campground is located in a transition zone between the two. Tenters will be happy campers in the regular campsites or the walk-in tent areas.

Turn off Soap Creek Road and descend into the upper loop that has six campsites. Occasional Ponderosa pines provide shade for the campsites, though some of the sites are in open sage land. The views from this hilltop are of spires and pinnacles—remnants of mudflow from an ancient volcano located across the Soap Creek Arm of Blue Mesa Reservoir. The horse corral in the middle of the loop indicates that this loop is popular with horse campers.

Continue down the steep gravel road to the middle loop. The first few sites are in open sage country above the lake, then come six walk-in tent sites. Park your car and head in for the short walk. Here, campsites are set into hills and on the hillsides, beneath shade-bearing trees. Soap Creek Arm of Blue Mesa Reservoir is just a stone's throw away and in view. The sites are wide-

CAMPGROUND RATINGS

Beauty: ★★★
Site privacy: ★★★
Site spaciousness: ★★★★
Quiet: ★★★
Security: ★★★★
Cleanliness/upkeep: ★★★

Stay in a walk-in tent site beside Colorado's biggest body of water at Curecanti National Recreation Area.

ly separated and situated to offer privacy, though a few are on the open side. This is the best area for tent camping. Five more traditional campsites are strung along the middle loop road.

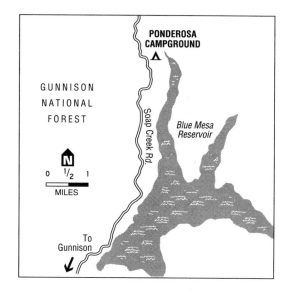

The lowest loop contains six more campsites in a treeless flat of sage. The austerity provides incredible views of the nearby reservoir and of Soap Creek.. Three walk-in sites are the closest to the reservoir. If you like to camp in view of the fascinating landscape, stay here, although the bathroom and spigot are a fair distance away at the boat ramp. The other loops have more convenient facilities.

This campground rarely fills, even on holidays. But the tent sites are the first to go, especially on the middle loop. For rustic solitude, this is the best camping at Curecanti, and you are well situated to enjoy the best of the recreation area and the West Elk.

Fishing and boating come naturally on the reservoir. Bank fishing is productive and popular in early summer for five species of trout. The boat launch here encourages bringing your own craft, but you can rent a boat at Lake Fork Marina 7 miles away. Leave the driving to others and take the boat tour of Morrow Point Reservoir. It's a mile walk down the 232 steps to the boat. Check out the Curecanti Spire in the upper Black Canyon of the Gunnison. Everyone comes back from this tour satisfied, and you get to work in a hike, too. If you want to boat Crystal Reservoir, an impoundment of the Gunnison River farther down, you have to carry your boat a good distance to put in.

You'll need to drive around the lake to enjoy the sights of Blue Mesa, a 20-mile-long reservoir with over 96 miles of shoreline. But the rock and water scenery merits a drive. On the lake you will see parasailers, fishermen, and boaters in varied craft. Waterskiing and swimming are usually limited to late August when the water is warmer.

History buffs will want to see the exhibit of the historic narrow-gauge train that ran through the canyon and the amazing story of the Gunnison Diversion Tunnel that continues to water the Uncompahgre Valley. Hikers can take the steep, 4-mile round-trip down Curecanti Creek to see the Curecanti Needle from another point. Check out the weird rock formations at Dillon Pinnacles. Leave the tent campground on the old road, cross Soap Creek on a footbridge, and walk the other side of the lake to the old Carpenter Homestead.

Other hikes can be found in the forested West Elk Wilderness. Rock formations jut out above the forests in this land, seldom traversed by humans. Use the Cow Creek and Coal Creek trails to form a loop hike starting at the Soap Creek Campground just up the road. Drive a distance up Soap Creek Road then hike up to Porcupine Cone. The West Elk is Colorado's unsung wilderness. Autumn will find hunters vying for the many elk that roam this land.

The Ponderosa Campground offers diversity not found at other places. It's like having two outdoor experiences in one trip.

To get there: From Gunnison, drive west on U.S. 50 for 24 miles to CO 92. Turn right on CO 92, cross Blue Mesa Dam, and continue 0.5 mile to Soap Creek Road. Turn right on Soap Creek Road and follow it for 7 miles to Ponderosa Campground.

KEY INFORMATION

Curecanti National Recreation Area, Ponderosa Campground
102 Elk Creek
Gunnison, CO 81230

Operated by: National Park Service

Information: (970) 641-2337 ext. 205; www.nps.gov/cure

Open: Mid-April through November

Individual sites: 29

Each site has: Picnic table, fire grate

Site assignment: First come, first serve; no reservation

Registration: Self-registration on site

Facilities: Water spigot, vault toilets, boat ramp, horse corral

Parking: At campsites and walk-in tent parking area

Fee: $10 per night mid-May through mid-September, $5 mid-April through mid-May and mid-September through mid-November

Elevation: 7,550 feet

Restrictions

Pets—On leash only

Fires—In fire grates only

Alcoholic beverages—Open containers not allowed in vehicles, except when parked at a campsite.

Vehicles—40 feet

Other—14-day stay limit

DOMINGUEZ CANYON

Grand Junction

L et's see . . . mountain biking, canyon hiking, trout fishing, scenic drives, Indian petroglyphs, mining ghost towns, canoeing the Gunnison River . . . all accessible from a free campground made for tent campers that happens to be one of the best in the state. This is Dominguez Canyon. Bureau of Land Management (BLM) campgrounds are generally less known to the public than national park and forest campgrounds. Once you find this little gem, you will be making return trips.

Drop off the Uncompahgre Plateau a bit and descend into Dominguez Canyon. Deep red cliffs are behind you. Below you, bordering Big Dominguez Creek, is a dense forest of large cottonwoods, complemented by thickets of willow and alder, making for a very green scene. Across the canyon, sage gives way to ponderosa pine and Douglas fir intermingling with piñon and juniper.

The air cools down as you approach the clear, chattering creek. Off to your right is a fenced-in grassy area below the cottonwoods. On the far side of a wood fence, three picnic tables lie astride the cool waters and offer creekside camping. The deep shade and the chilled air along the creek makes a great escape from the heat of the summer sun in the Colorado River Valley. Farther on, just across the shallow ford of Big Dominguez Creek, lies a single site in the very thick of the cottonwoods. This campsite is for privacy lovers.

CAMPGROUND RATINGS

Beauty: ★★★★
Site privacy: ★★★
Site spaciousness: ★★★★
Quiet: ★★★★
Security: ★★★
Cleanliness/upkeep: ★★★

Enjoy both the red canyons and green forests of the Uncompahgre Plateau from Big Dominguez.

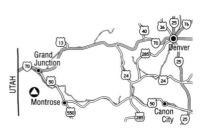

Just upstream from this secluded campsite is a small footbridge connecting both sides of the campground. The entrance road fords the creek and to your right is a small meadow and parking area. An attractive log fence guards more campsites. The cottonwoods here are smaller, still providing ample shade, but letting campers enjoy the views around them. Small openings in the fence allow campers to access sites on the far side, which allows for tent-only camping. The brush rises high enough to make for good campsite privacy.

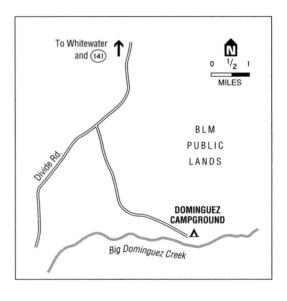

Three of the five campsites have two picnic tables each, allowing for larger parties. One campsite is far back in the woods and looks over a mesa that comes to a point above Big Dominguez Creek and an unnamed tributary.

Two other parties joined me on my stay. The small campground rarely fills, so make your plans and come on up. There is no water provided, though springwater from a pipe is located on the entrance road just above the campground. You could also use the water from Big Dominguez Creek and treat it. Two new vault toilets have been put in on both sides of the creek.

The campground is perched on the edge of the 70,000-acre Big Dominguez Wilderness Study Area. The BLM expects this area ultimately to become a full-fledged wilderness. One look and you'll agree that it should be preserved.

A good way to get that look is on the Big Dominguez Trail, which starts at the campground. You can head down the canyon and enumerate reasons for preservation. On the lower part of the canyon are Indian petroglyphs; the best way to access the cliff drawings is from Cactus Park. Watch for the sign for

Cactus Park on Colorado 141 as you head for the campground, then take the trail toward Triangle Mesa and take the right split down to the Big Dom-inguez Creek and the petroglyphs. You can also follow the Smith Point Trail up Dominguez Canyon from the campground.

If you like fishing small creeks for trout as much as I do, you'll love Big Dominguez Creek. Take the Big Doming-uez Trail down the canyon and simply drop into the creek drainage, then work your way up—secretively I might add—and cast with small spinners. Rainbow trout will positively attack your lure. If you want to ride in the water instead of walking through it, check with outfitters in Whitewater and Grand Junction. The nearby Gunnison River offers some decent canoeing that is more of a relaxed float than a hair-raising whitewater ride.

Mountain bikers take note that the heart of the 140-mile Tabeguache Trail passes right through this campground. You can take the trail up to the plateau or drop down toward Cactus Park. Send for a map of the Tabeguache Trail from the BLM office in Grand Junction.

Auto tourists will want to return to CO 141 and drive farther up Unaweep Can-yon toward Gateway. In the mountains east of Gateway, many old mining sites and miners shacks are on BLM lands. Again, inquire at the BLM office for details; you'll like what they have to offer in this part of the state.

To get there: From Grand Junction, drive southeast on U.S. 50 for 10 miles to CO 141 and the town of Whitewater. Turn right on CO 141 and follow it for 11.5 miles to Divide Road. Turn left on Divide Road and follow it for 5 miles to a fork in the road. Turn left at the fork. There is a sign and arrow saying "Big Dominguez Resource Conservation Area." Follow this road 5

KEY INFORMATION

Dominguez Campground
2815 H Road
Grand Junction, CO 81506

Operated by: Bureau of Land Management

Information: (970) 244-3000; www.co.blm.gov/gjra/gjra. htm

Open: Mid-May through mid-October

Individual sites: 9

Each site has: Picnic table, fire ring

Site assignment: First come, first served; no reservation

Registration: No registration

Facilities: Vault toilets (no water)

Parking: At tent camping park-ing areas

Fee: None

Elevation: 7,500 feet

Restrictions

Pets—On leash only

Fires—In fire rings only

Alcoholic beverages—At camp-sites only

Vehicles—None

Other—14-day stay limit

ELBERT CREEK

Leadville

A ctive campers come to Elbert Creek, and it seems that they are not around enough to really take in the atmosphere of the campground. Elbert Creek has an agreeable location, high in the mountains along a resonant stream, where you really get a sense of being away from it all. But campers here seem to think they are near it all, at least those exercise-oriented pastimes that active campers like. Hiking is the main exercise; Mount Elbert and the Mount Massive Wilderness are just a walk away from the campground.

There are lakes and streams nearby for fishing. Mountain bikers like to pedal up to the Mount Champion Mill and the Colorado Trail, which is the backbone of the state's trail system. Somehow, campers find time to eat, sleep, and rest a little before going at it again the next day.

Elbert Creek is a small campground laid out underneath a lodgepole pine forest in a flat along Halfmoon Creek. Enter the campground and the road splits into two drives running parallel to Halfmoon Creek that have vehicle turnarounds at their ends. This avails more streamside campsites. The forest is virtually devoid of ground cover, save for a few small saplings and rocks. However, the brush thickens alongside Halfmoon Creek, which flows loud and clear below the campground.

The right-hand drive has nine campsites. Many of these sites are spread far back in

CAMPGROUND RATINGS

Beauty: ★★★★
Site privacy: ★★★
Site spaciousness: ★★★★★
Quiet: ★★★
Security: ★★★
Cleanliness/upkeep: ★★★

You can walk from your tent and climb Mount Elbert, Colorado's highest peak at 14, 433 feet.

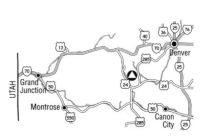

the woods. Four of the campsites are streamside and offer solitude. The left-hand drive has eight campsites that are very large, but three of them are a little close to the forest road that runs by the campground. Avoid the last three campsites unless you want to see who is driving by.

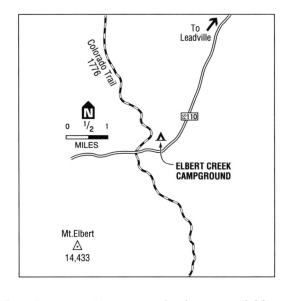

The pump well and vault toilets are conveniently in between the two drives. Elbert Creek receives heavy weekend use from hikers, so try to get there on Friday night or early Saturday if you are a weekend warrior. Otherwise, campsites are nearly always available.

Hikers love to bag peaks here in the Centennial State, and the highest point in Colorado, Mount Elbert, is very close. Elbert is the second highest point in the lower 48 states, behind Mount Whitney in California. It is a 3.5-mile climb to the crest from the nearby trailhead. There's nothing technical about this well-marked and maintained trail, though snow may present a problem even in the early summer. You can also make a loop hike from here using the North Mount Elbert, South Mount Elbert, and Colorado trails.

Just a short walk up the road is the Mount Massive Wilderness. Much of this wilderness is above the timber line, so bring adequate clothing for inclement weather. Mount Massive is the second highest peak in Colorado, only 12 feet lower than Mount Elbert. You can stay at Elbert Creek and bag the two highest peaks in the state. Just beyond the Mount Elbert trailhead, take the Colorado Trail north into the wilderness up to the Mount Massive Trail and hike to the peak. You can also climb to the North Halfmoon Lakes using Trail #1485, which starts up Forest Service Road 110 a couple of miles. Farther up this same road is the Champion Mine, with its aerial tramway still intact. You can bike or drive to the Champion Mine.

The Iron Mike Mine site is a hike or bike up South Halfmoon Creek. Nearby Emerald Lake, which also features a picnic area, offers fishing, as does all the previously mentioned creeks. Speaking of fish, you ought to check out the Leadville National Fish Hatchery. Established in 1889, it is the second oldest federal fish hatchery in the country. Fish from here have been placed all over the Rockies, and today it still produces brook, cutthroat trout, and rainbow trout. There are trails on the hatchery grounds as well, with great views of the big mountains you came here to climb.

To get there: From Leadville, head south on U.S. 24 for 4 miles to CR 110 and the sign for the Leadville National Fish Hatchery. Turn right here and follow CR 110 for 0.7 mile to Halfmoon Creek Road. Turn left on Halfmoon Creek Road and follow it a short ways before the sharp right turn to stay on Halfmoon Creek Road. Continue on Halfmoon Creek Road as it turns to FS 110. Elbert Creek Campground will be 4 miles up on your right.

KEY INFORMATION

Elbert Creek Campground
Leadville Ranger District
2015 North Poplar
Leadville, CO 80461

Operated by: U.S. Forest Service

Information: (719) 486-0749; www.fs.fed.us/r2/psicc/leadvile

Open: June through Labor Day

Individual sites: 17

Each site has: Picnic table, fire grate

Site assignment: First come, first served; no reservation

Registration: Self-registration on site

Facilities: Pump well, vault toilet, trash collection

Parking: At campsites only

Fee: $9 per night, $4.50 per additional vehicle

Elevation: 10,100 feet

Restrictions

Pets—On leash only

Fires—In fire grates only

Alcoholic beverages—At campsites only

Vehicles—16 feet

Other—14-day stay limit

FULFORD CAVE

Eagle

There's one really good thing about staying at Fulford Cave Campground: If it rains, you aren't necessarily tent-bound. You can take advantage of rainy time as a chance to explore Fulford Cave itself, which is less than a mile from this intimate campground. Fulford Cave Campground is in an unusual setting and has other trails leading into the western side of the Holy Cross Wilderness, one of Colorado's best wild places.

The hilltop campground is on the left flank of the East Brush Creek Valley, in a scattered forest of aspen, spruce, and fir. Directly up the watershed is Craig Peak. Below you is the meadow of Yeoman Park. Off to your right, a few hundred feet down a steep rockslide, is East Brush Creek. Just behind the campground is a beaver pond. Off to your left is the trailhead to Fulford Cave and the other trails leading into the Holy Cross Wilderness.

As the forest road dead ends, the campground is straight ahead and the Fulford Cave trailhead parking is off to your left. A small spur road splits to the right, where the first three campsites lie. The first one is right on the edge of the drop into East Brush Creek. Be careful after dark if you camp here. The other two sites are by themselves and out of view over a little knob; they offer the most in campsite privacy.

The other four campsites are on a little loop road just as you pull up. One site is in

CAMPGROUND RATINGS

Beauty: ★★★
Site privacy: ★★★
Site spaciousness: ★★
Quiet: ★★★★
Security: ★★★
Cleanliness/upkeep: ★★★

Fulford Cave offers attractions both above and below ground. The camping is above ground.

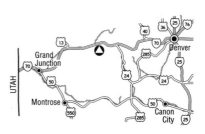

71

the center of the loop, along with the vault toilet. Two water spigots are available at this diminutive campground. No self-respecting RV or pop-up camper would try to fit in these tent-only campsites. The bigger rigs stay just down the road at Yeoman Park Campground, where you should camp if Fulford Cave ever fills (which it rarely does).

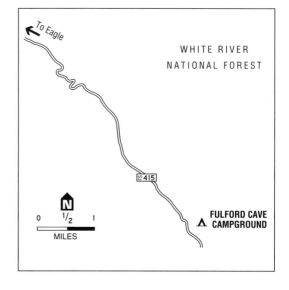

Fulford Cave is Colorado's eighth-largest cavern. Over 2,600 square feet of the underground location has been plotted. Inside are big rooms, narrow crevices, streams, stalagmites, and stalactites. (Harken back to your school days and try to remember which one develops from the top down and which one builds from the bottom up.) Fulford Cave was discovered during the mining boom of the nineteenth century by a man named Maxwell, who named the cave after the nearby mining town of Fulford. He never found the riches he sought in the cave, but he did leave a timbered entrance and a pit entrance.

The 0.7-mile trail to the cave starts by the gate at the trailhead parking area. Start making your way up the forest on switchbacks, and you'll soon come to the cave. If you do explore inside the cave, the Forest Service recommends you have the following with you: durable and warm clothing, gloves, hard hat, flashlights and head lamps, sturdy boots, and drinking water. A cave map is available at the Ranger Station in Eagle. Remember, just like on the surface, you are responsible for your own safety in the cave.

Speaking of on the surface, there are two good trails that head into the Holy Cross Wilderness from Fulford Cave. They both lead to 16-acre Lake Charles.

The Lake Charles Trail follows East Brush Creek for 4.4 miles before coming to the lake. Mystic Island Lake is a mile farther. Both lakes offer good fishing for cutthroat trout, while East Brush Creek offers fishing for rainbow, brook, and brown trout. I recommend fishing the stream in the meadows and beaver ponds below Fulford Cave.

The Ironedge Trail is a horse and foot trail. It offers many highlights on its seven-mile journey, as the surroundings change from aspen to fir to alpine tundra above the tree line. Along the way are cabins, meadows, and mine sites, interspersed with good views. The last two miles are downhill to Lake Charles. You can combine the Ironedge Trail with the Lake Charles Trail to make an excellent loop hike. For this particular adventure, you don't need a hardhat.

KEY INFORMATION

Fulford Cave Campground
Eagle Ranger District
P.O. Box 720, 125 West 5th Street
Eagle, CO 81631

Operated by: U.S. Forest Service

Information: (970) 328-6388; www.wildernet.com

Open: July through October

Individual sites: 7

Each site has: Picnic table, fire pit

Site assignment: First come, first served; no reservation

Registration: Self-registration on site

Facilities: Water spigot, vault toilet, summer trash collection

Parking: At campsites only

Fee: $8 per night

Elevation: 9,400 feet

Restrictions

Pets—On leash only

Fires—In fire pits only

Alcoholic beverages—At campsites only

Vehicles—25 feet

Other—14-day stay limit

To get there: From the I-70 exit in Eagle, head south on U.S. 6 as it veers right and then make a sharp left on Capitol Street. Proceed on Capitol Street as it turns into Brush Creek Road for 10 miles and come to FS 415 (East Brush Creek Road). Turn left on FS 415 and follow it 7 miles to Fulford Cave Campground.

GENEVA PARK

Grant

Geneva Park Campground was constructed by Forest Service volunteers in 1981. Not only did they produce a fine campground but they also chose their site well. The actual site is in a mildly rolling pine forest in the high country of the northern Pike National Forest. A mere 26 campsites are spread over a fair size of woodland. The location is ideal for exploring the Mount Evans Wilderness, which is less than a mile to the east.

At the head of the actual meadow of Geneva Park an unbroken stand of lodgepole pine grows. Their straight trunks, once used as tent poles for the lodges of western Indian tribes, form a beautiful sight when growing in dense stands as they do here at the campground. Most of the trees here don't have any branches on the lower part of their trunk, then they all seem to sprout branches lush with green needles, contrasting with their reddish-brown patterned bark. Their fallen needles lie on the ground, forming a dusky carpet among the scattered stones. I am sorry to report that some of these lodgepoles had to be cut down because of a dwarf mistletoe parasitic infestation, but the vast majority of trees remains to form an attractive landscape for your camping experience.

Cross Smelter Creek on a bridge, then come to the campground. Here, you will see the more open forest and some stumps of the trees that were cut down to keep the

CAMPGROUND RATINGS

Beauty: ★★★★
Site privacy: ★★★
Site spaciousness: ★★★
Quiet: ★★★★
Security: ★★★
Cleanliness/upkeep: ★★★

The Mount Evans Wilderness is just a hike away from Geneva Park.

forest healthy. In spite of the cutting, the campsites here have adequate shade. These sites are closest to the pump well.

The actual loop begins after the first seven campsites. The road splits off to the right, just past the newly installed vault toilet. Campsites beneath the lodgepoles are either higher or lower than the road, depending on the variation of the terrain. As the loop swings around, there are three campsites that lie under the lodgepole and

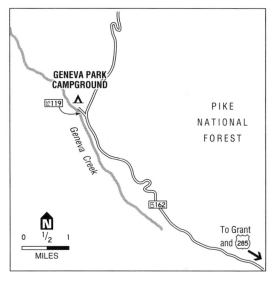

border their own private meadow opposite the campground road. Beyond the meadow campsites, other campsites outside the loop climb up a hill.

This is the least used of the three campgrounds in the Geneva Creek valley. It normally doesn't fill on weekends or even most holidays. You should be able to get a campsite here on all but the busiest traditional holidays.

It's only a 15-minute walk to one of the trailheads to the Mount Evans Wilderness; it's a short drive to the other two entry points to the 74,000-acre preserve that was designated one year before Geneva Pass Campground came to be. Within the wilderness are two fourteeners and a rare type of arctic tundra, normally found only within the boundaries of the Arctic Circle. Small pools of water form a plant community unlike the normally dry, brittle Colorado alpine tundra. Mountain goats and bighorn sheep are at home here in this challenging environment.

There are three convenient points of entry to the wilderness for Geneva Park campers. Farther up County Road 62 is Guanella Pass at 11,669 feet. It's the easiest way to get high. Just south of Geneva Park you will find the Abyss

Trail comencement. This trail climbs strenuously along the glacier-carved valley of Scott Gomer Creek for 7 miles to Abyss Lake. The lake lies perched in a cirque, an encircling wall of rock, with Mount Bierstadt on one side and Mount Evans on the other. Farther south on CR 62 is the Threemile Trail. It heads east into the wilderness toward Tahana Mountain and can be used in combination with the Rosalie and Abyss Trails to form a loop, if you don't mind a bit of road walking.

I enjoy camping in varied forest types. At Geneva Park you can have the lodgepole pine camping experience, then go have the Mount Evans Wilderness hiking experience.

KEY INFORMATION

Geneva Park Campground
South Platte Ranger District
19316 Goddard Ranch Court
Morrison, CO 80465

Operated by: U.S. Forest Service

Information: (303) 275-5610; www.fs.fed.us/r2/psicc/spl

Open: May through October

Individual sites: 26

Each site has: Picnic table, fire ring

Site assignment: First come, first served; no reservation

Registration: By phone (call (877) 444-6777) or self-registration on site

Facilities: Hand-pump well, vault toilets

Parking: At campsites only

Fee: $11 per night

Elevation: 9,800 feet

Restrictions

Pets—On leash only

Fires—In fire rings only

Alcoholic beverages—At campsites only

Vehicles—20 feet

Other—14-day stay limit

To get there: From U.S. 285 in Grant, head north on CR 62 toward Guanella Pass for 6 miles, then veer left on FS 119 and follow it for 0.4 mile to Geneva Park Campground, which will be on your left.

GOLD PARK

Minturn

Gold Park is nearly the ideal tent campground. It is somewhat out of the way, on a dirt road, small, in a picturesque setting, and adjacent to many outdoor attractions. The dirt road leads up Homestake Valley, a scenic watershed in the Sawatch Range. Gold Park, with only 11 campsites, is located along Homestake Creek, which is hemmed in by Homestake and Whitney peaks. These mountains are protected as part of the Holy Cross Wilderness. This wilderness area, like most, offers the best recreation of the national forests, mountain biking excepted. Several trailheads are a short drive away. The historic mining town of Holy Cross City is a 4-mile walk, or a rugged four-wheel-drive trip away. Homestake Reservoir and Homestake Creek offer some decent fishing.

Gold Park is set in a wooded flat between Homestake Creek and a low-lying hill covered in trees and boulders. Beyond the pay station the drive veers to the right, passing the campground host in the first campsite. Lodgepole pine and other smaller conifers shade the entire campsite. Large, spacious camping areas are spread along the loop as you proceed up the gravel drive, which then veers left as the rocky hill pinches in the flat toward the Homestake Creek.

The campsites come closer to the road as the vehicle turnaround approaches, where there are three of the best campsites. One is snug against a shaded rock outcrop, and

CAMPGROUND RATINGS

Beauty: ★★★★★
Site privacy: ★★★
Site spaciousness: ★★★★★
Quiet: ★★★★
Security: ★★★★
Cleanliness/upkeep: ★★★★

Mine yourself a good time at Gold Park.

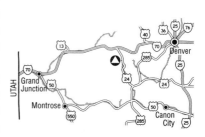

the other two lie next to Homestake Creek. These last two campsites are the biggest and most coveted sites at Gold Park, which is a well-kept, clean campground.

Water spigots and a vault toilet serve this quaint camping area. Gold Park receives moderate use, filling up on the usual holidays. About the only RV you will see here is the campground host. It is unusual, but good, to have a host in a campground this small. The mood here is serene, with the creek providing a naturally symphonic backdrop.

The upper part of this valley was once home to the mining town of Holy Cross City. The first mines were staked in 1880; Gold Park Mining Company was formed in 1881. The ore assays promised a boom. However, the outer layer of ore proved to be the richest, and the gold wasn't nearly as rich at deeper levels. By 1884, it was finally admitted that the mine was a bust. Another attempt was made in the same area in 1896; a deep tunnel was dug, but the profit just wasn't there. You can take Forest Service Road 759 up to the site of this mine by foot, bike, or jeep. These days, your only strikes will be from fish on Homestake Creek or Homestake Reservoir, 3 miles up FS 703, your route to Gold Park. The lake is 480 acres in size and is brimming with trout.

Take time to explore the Holy Cross Wilderness, whose waters are coveted by Colorado Springs. However, development plans have been halted for the wilderness-that-almost-wasn't due to the city tampering with the natural flows. Today, you can enjoy the wilderness's alpine lakes and icy streams. The Fall Creek Trail starts about 2 miles up the road to Holy Cross City. The trail heads up to Hunky Dory Lake and the stair-stepping Seven Sisters Lakes, where rock cliffs make for watery backdrops.

It's a 1,500-foot climb in 3 miles on the Missouri Lakes Trail. The trail starts up FS 704 and goes above the timber line. A shorter walk to a high-country lake is the Fancy Pass Trail, which also starts off of FS 704 above Gold Park. Pass some dams that you would be seeing all over the place if Colorado Springs had had its way, then steeply make your way to Fancy Lake at 2 miles. Treasure Vault Lake is another mile beyond, though you have to go over Fancy Pass, and it is downhill to the lake.

Down from Gold Park is the Whitney Lake Trail, which offers views on its 2.3-mile journey to Whitney Lake. From here you can scale 13,271-foot Mount Whitney, rising on the north shore of the lake, if you follow the west ridge to the top. No matter where you go in the Holy Cross Wilderness, appreciate it, because it almost never came into existence.

KEY INFORMATION

Gold Park Campground
Holy Cross Ranger District
24747 U.S. Highway 24
Minturn, CO 81645

Operated by: U.S. Forest Service

Information: (970) 827-5715; www.wildernet.com

Open: June through September

Individual sites: 11

Each site has: Picnic table, fire grate

Site assignment: First come, first served; no reservation

Registration: Self-registration on site

Facilities: Water spigot, vault toilets, trash collection

Parking: At campsites only

Fee: $10 per night

Elevation: 9,300 feet

Restrictions

  Pets—On leash only

  Fires—In fire grates only

  Alcoholic beverages—At campsites only

  Vehicles—40 feet

  Other—10-day stay limit

To get there: From I-70 near Minturn, head south on U.S. 24 for 11.5 miles to FS 703 (Homestake Road). Turn right on FS 703 and follow it for 7 miles to Gold Park Campground, which will be on your left.

KITE LAKE

Fairplay

You can bag three fourteeners in one hike from this campground, which lies above the tree line in a bowl of granite mountains. This is also a historic mining district that you can tour by car. But before you load your tent in the car, call ahead to check if the campground is open and on the road conditions leading to the campground. Forest personnel try to have Kite Lake open by the beginning of June, but sometimes the snowpack just won't allow it. Long, harsh winters at this altitude can be rough on a gravel road, so it may take a while to get the road open for travel. Most passenger cars can make the drive to the lake; however there are two fords on the road, the second of which can be a foot or more deep. However, if worst comes to worst, you can park at the ford and walk the last few hundred yards to the campground in this land of extremes. Not only is the area historic, the campground unique, and three fourteeners accessible, but the Windy Ridge Scenic Area is nearby, with bristlecone pines that are among the world's oldest living organisms.

Mount Buckskin, Mount Democrat, Mount Lincoln, and Mount Bross look down on your tent as it lies along chilly Kite Lake in the alpine tundra, where nothing grows taller than knee-high. Outward, the Buckskin Creek drainage affords views into the "lowlands" below.

The first set of campsites are on your left as you drive up. One site is in plain view,

CAMPGROUND RATINGS

Beauty:	★★★★★
Site privacy:	★★
Site spaciousness:	★★★★★
Quiet:	★★★
Security:	★★★
Cleanliness/upkeep:	★★★

Kite Lake, at 12,000 feet, is the highest campsite in this entire guidebook.

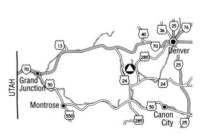

another is near the new
vault toilet, and a third is
toward the lake over a
small, rocky knoll. This last
one offers the only thing
resembling privacy here.
Cross the outlet for Kite
Lake and come to the other
two campsites in a flat beside the lake. Everything is
out in the open. Spaciousness is at the maximum, just
as privacy is next to nil, but
with such a great view, who
wants to be hemmed in by
trees anyway?

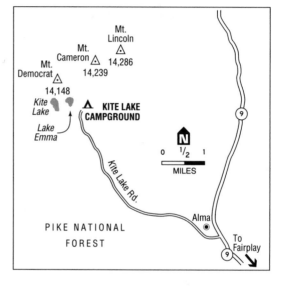

Now that you have your
warmest sleeping bag, all
the fleece you own, and lots of hot chocolate, sit back, admire the view, and
decide what to do first. If you want to climb the fourteeners, give yourself six
hours to do it. Head north from the lake and climb to a gap where you can
look down and see how Kite Lake got its name. Turn left on the ridge line to
bag Mount Democrat, then come back to the gap. This time, head right up to
Mount Lincoln around Mount Cameron. The drop is severe from the top of
Mount Lincoln on the other side. Backtrack again to Cameron, then head
southeast to Bross, which has a flat top. Look for all the mine sites. Then carefully drop down the talus slopes leading down to Kite Lake. Leave early in the
morning to avoid getting trapped by afternoon thunderstorms.

Back down the main road is the marked forest road to Windy Ridge. Follow
this road up to the Windy Ridge Scenic Area. These strong winds that give the
area its name contort the ancient bristlecone pines into shapes that you must
see to believe. It's hard enough to believe these trees can survive up here at
all. These bristlecone pines survive through the ages because they resist fire
by being spread apart, and they go nearly dormant during abnormally harsh

or dry years. When you look at these trees, imagine living on this mountain for 2,000 years.

You'll also want to take the Buckskin Gulch auto tour. It chronicles the mining history of the Kite Lake drainage. While driving up along Buckskin Creek to the lake, you will notice the former mines high on the surrounding slopes. Get your pamphlet at the Ranger Station in Fairplay. See the cemetery and the site of the former settlement of Buckskin Joe, once home to several thousand folks. Learn about how the ore was separated, the history of the old buildings, the life of miners and their families, and about mining in the area today. And you thought tent camping at this elevation could be challenging!

Seriously, do bring warm clothes, sunscreen, and an adventurous attitude. You will reap some lasting memories of your camping experience at Kite Lake.

KEY INFORMATION

Kite Lake Campground
South Platte Ranger District
P.O. Box 219
Fairplay, CO 80440

Operated by: U.S. Forest Service

Information: (719) 836-2031; www.fs.fed.us/r2/psicc/sopa

Open: June through September

Individual Sites: 7

Each site has: Picnic table, fire ring

Site assignment: First come, first served; no reservation

Registration: Self-registration on site

Facilities: Vault toilet (bring your own water)

Parking: At campsites only

Fee: $7 per night

Elevation: 12,000 feet

Restrictions

Pets—On leash only

Fires—In fire rings only

Alcoholic beverages—At campsites only

Vehicles—No trailers allowed

Other—14-day stay limit

To get there: From the Ranger Station in Fairplay, drive north on CO 9 for 8miles to the town of Alma. Turn left on CR 8 (Kite Lake Road) and follow it 6 miles to the dead end at Kite Lake Campground.

LOST LAKE

Paonia

The setting at Lost Lake Campground is classic. A shimmering jewel of water is perched high in the mountains with a forested backdrop, from which snowy, granite twin peaks rise majestically. Most of the campsites have views of this inspiring sight, as if the Kebler Pass Road wasn't scenic enough on the way up to Lost Lake. Rising out of the West Elk Wilderness, East Beckwith and West Beckwith mountains form twin sentinels over Lost Lake Slough, the body of water beside which you camp. The actual Lost Lake is farther up in the mountains, less than a mile distant.

Not only do you have some of the most scenic tent camping in Colorado, you are also within a mile of two wilderness areas: the West Elk and the Raggeds Wilderness to your north, which those pointed peaks off to your left as you drove up. So if you get bored with relaxing and fishing at Lost Lake, there are nearly 300 miles of trails between the two wilderness areas on which to exhaust yourself.

When you finally make it to Lost Lake Slough, veer left; to your right are some Forest Service–owned cabins. No need to register or pay, the camping here is free. The main drive runs between the lake, and the first two campsites are large and have popular lake views. Then pass the pump well, which probably won't be working; bring your own water. Then come a few campsites that are directly lakeside on

CAMPGROUND RATINGS

Beauty: ★★★★★
Site privacy: ★★★
Site spaciousness: ★★★
Quiet: ★★★★
Security: ★★★
Cleanliness/upkeep: ★★★

The view here is so good that the Forest Service should charge a fee instead of letting you camp for free.

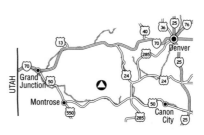

some less-than-level ter-
rain. The view from here,
however, may be worth a
sloping night in the tent.

Beyond this, come to the
campground drive, which
leads away from the lake
onto a hill wooded with
conifers. The shade is welcome here on those relent-
less summer days, and the
privacy is enhanced by the
trees; however, your view of
the mountains and lake is
obstructed. A small mead-
ow slopes off the drive at the
turnaround. You pass one
campsite in the center of the

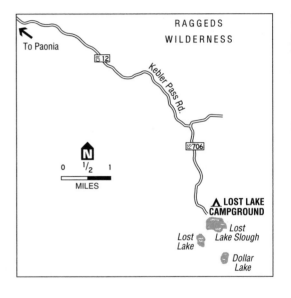

turnaround that is convenient to the vault toilet and one more campsite
downslope in the woods opposite the lake. This last campsite is generally the
last to be taken.

Later on in the summer, Lost Lake will fill up on weekends. Earlier in the
season, the weather can be chancy here. As always, call ahead before making
the long drive to camp here or anywhere. The campground opening is depen-
dent on the snow up here. The Forest Service will open the campground as
soon as the road is open. If the campground is open, you should have no trouble finding a campsite on a weekday.

The serrated, prominent spires of the Ruby Range give the Raggeds
Wilderness its name. Aspens and conifers grace the lower, wooded slopes.
Trails lead into this land off Kebler Pass Road, both before and after the
turnoff to Lost Lake Campground. On your way up, you passed the trailhead
for Trail #836, which leads down Trout Creek. To enjoy the higher alpine
country, drive toward Kebler Pass and head north on Trail #830, which passes a few lakes as it runs parallel to the Ruby Range.

A short walk away from the campgrounds is the Beckwith Pass Trail, which heads south into the 17,600-acre West Elk Wilderness. Your hike leads south to Beckwith Pass, which isn't usually passable until mid-July. It is a little more than 2 miles to the pass. From there, you can split left to the Cliff Creek Trail, which is actually just before the pass, or continue into the heart of the West Elk. Allow yourself ample time to return before dark.

Closer to home is the Three Lakes Trail, which departs from the campground. It offers a 3-mile loop hike that extends to the timber line and passes the actual Lost Lake and Dollar Lake. The views of the Beckwiths are better than the fishing on these upper lakes. The fishing at Lost Lake Slough is considerably better, as it is better fishing to begin with and is also periodically restocked. You can either bank fish or get onto the lake in any hand-propelled craft. No motors are allowed.

KEY INFORMATION

Lost Lake Campground
Paonia Ranger District
P.O. Box 1030
Paonia, CO 81428
Operated by: U.S. Forest Service
Information: (970) 527-4131; www.fs.fed.us/r2/gmug
Open: Mid-May through mid-November
Individual sites: 11
Each site has: Picnic table, fire grate
Site assignment: First come, first served; no reservations
Registration: No registration
Facilities: Vault toilets (no water)
Parking: At campsites only
Fee: No fee
Elevation: 9,600 feet
Restrictions
  Pets—On leash only
  Fires—In fire grates only
  Alcoholic beverages—At campsites only
  Vehicles—16 feet
  Other—14-day stay limit

To get there: From Paonia, drive north on CO 133 to CR 12 (Kebler Pass Road). The sign at the right turn will say "Crested Butte." Turn right on Kebler Pass Road and follow it for 16 miles to FS 706. Turn right on FS 706 and drive 2 more miles to Lost Lake Campground.

LOST PARK

Jefferson

L ost Park Campground sits atop a knoll in the large valley at the confluence of Indian Creek, North Fork Lost Creek, and South Fork Lost Creek. The Kenosha and Tarryall Mountains serve as your campground cathedrals. It is in this enhanced setting that you can set up your tent, then fish, hike, and explore the Lost Creek Wilderness until the call of civilization rings too loud to ignore.

You won't want to leave this small, hilltop campground cloaked in lodgepole pine and complemented by other conifers. With only 12 campsites and nearly 20 miles of dirt road, civilization doesn't exactly come knocking on your tent flap. Two drives with vehicle turnarounds at their ends divide the campsites, which are spread very far apart.

The first drive circles the top of the knoll. Most of the campsites are on the more heavily wooded left side, while the few on the right look over Lost Creek below and Bison Peak above. A campsite lies in the rocky center of the auto turnaround. Other boulders serve as landscaping car barriers.

The lower drive turns left and drops down toward the North Fork of Lost Creek. Two campsites lie on a slope to your left. Stay here if you don't mind sleeping a little tilted. Pass the northbound section of the Brookside-McCurdy Trail. Follow the drive as it swings right along the creek, passing the well pump in a meadow and a

CAMPGROUND RATINGS

Beauty: ★★★★
Site privacy: ★★★★
Site spaciousness: ★★★★
Quiet: ★★★★
Security: ★★★
Cleanliness/upkeep: ★★★

Lost Park is your camping ticket to the Lost Creek Wilderness.

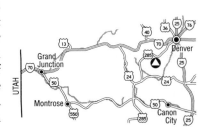

lonesome campsite on your right that offers the maximum in privacy. The drive continues past other campsites that sit on a small hill looking downstream on Lost Creek. These sites also have other conifers in addition to the lodgepole. Then you come to the vehicle turnaround with one more large campsite on your right.

There is one set of vault toilets for each gender at each loop. But bigger amenities, such as three fishable streams and three trailheads at the campground, will make you

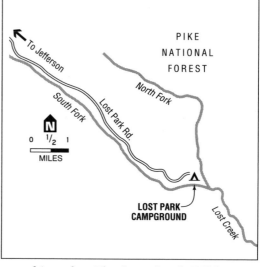

appreciate Lost Park more than anything else. The Lost Creek Wilderness, which is most of the land you see around you, is almost 120,000 acres of meadows, woods, and unusual granite formations, where one of Colorado's largest herds of bighorn sheep live. There are nearly 100 miles of trails to enjoy, and you probably can get most of the hiking you desire without restarting your vehicle until it is time to head home. After all, a wilderness is defined as an untrammeled place where man is just a visitor. And visit you must.

The Wigwam Trail heads east along Lost Creek proper. Soon you'll come to the very large East Lost Park. This is a huge meadow that goes on and on. Veer right on an unmaintained fishing trail if you want to keep going down Lost Creek. The Wigwam Trail follows a feeder stream up and over a divide to the Wigwam Creek drainage.

The north end of the Brookside-McCurdy Trail skirts the wilderness; mountain bikers can pedal this section. It then intersects the Colorado Trail, where you can veer right into the wilderness high country or veer left and keep on biking to the top, over to the Craig Creek drainage. If you go south on the Brookside-McCurdy Trail from the campground, you will head up Indian Creek toward Bison Pass. There are fishable waters with small, but spunky trout ready to tear at your lure on all the creeks.

Mountain bikers can't enter the wilderness, but they do have their own trails to use just back down Forest Service Road 56. Walleye Gulch Road and Topaz Road, FS 854 and FS 446, respectively, can be used with other connecting forest service roads to make loops. I recommend that hikers, bikers, and fishermen all get the Trails Illustrated map titled "Tarryall Mountains, Kenosha Pass," for the general area. Get all your supplies before you get anywhere near the area; Lost Park is far from the main roads. The nearby towns are small and don't have much in the way of supplies except for the convenience store variety. One more thing, bring your binoculars to help you spot bighorn sheep.

To get there: From Jefferson, drive north 1 mile to CR 56 (Lost Park Road), turn right and drive east for 19 miles to the dead end at Lost Park Campground.

KEY INFORMATION

Lost Park Campground
South Park Ranger District
P.O. Box 219
Fairplay, CO 80440

Operated by: U.S. Forest Service

Information: (719) 836-2031; www.fs.fed.us/r2/psicc/sopa

Open: June through September

Individual sites: 12

Each site has: Picnic table, fire grate

Site assignment: First come, first served; no reservation

Registration: Self-registration on site

Facilities: Hand-pump well, vault toilets

Parking: At campsites only

Fee: $7 per night

Elevation: 10,000 feet

Restrictions

Pets—On leash only

Fires—In fire grates only

Alcoholic beverages—At campsites only

Vehicles—22 feet

Other—14-day stay limit

MIRROR LAKE

Almont

Perched on the western edge of the Continental Divide, Mirror Lake reflects the snow and granite Rocky Mountains rimmed in verdant forests that colorfully contrast with the Colorado blue sky. Here you can come to escape the stress of modern civilization and reflect on the restorative qualities that a day, a week, or a weekend in our grand national forests can have on your attitude. Mirror Lake Campground is just such a place to seek your scenic respite.

While climbing sharply in your car along East Willow Creek, appreciate not only the beauty of the region but the fact that you can access this high lake without having to walk all your supplies in. The road becomes very steep just before arriving at the lake. Make your right turn into the campground and climb another hill. Campsites appear to the left of the road in a stand of spruce, hidden from the water. Then you pop out on a small hill and the lake comes into view. The wind was calm on my visit, and the lake lived up to its name, reflecting Fitzpatrick Peak, Tincup Pass, and Emma Burr Mountain.

What was strange, though, was the state of the campground and lake—they were deserted. Such splendor with only me to appreciate it, although granted, it was a weekday. There were many favorable campsites as I drove through the loop. Several campsites were right on the lake,

CAMPGROUND RATINGS

Beauty: ★★★★
Site privacy: ★★★
Site spaciousness: ★★★
Quiet: ★★★★
Security: ★★★
Cleanliness/upkeep: ★★★

Mirror Lake offers a restful alpine setting for tent campers who want to escape the summer heat of the valleys.

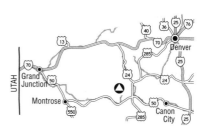

albeit a bit sun-drenched. Others were set off in the woods with partial views of the lake. Though the amenities here are minimal (only vault toilets, you must bring your own water), the perk of easy access to an attractive, high lake right on the divide should attract more campers. The rough road and 16-foot vehicle length limit deters nearly all folks except for determined tent campers. Mirror Lake does get some weekend business, especially later in the summer. This

same high elevation that lends such beauty also keeps campers from wandering up here in June because of the uncertainty of whether the campground is even open. Call ahead before you make the drive to Mirror Lake.

If you continue forward instead of veering right into the campground, you will come to the boat launch and parking area. The road that traces the left bank of the lake is the rough, four-wheel-drive road over 12,154-foot-high Tincup Pass. Only hand-propelled craft are allowed onto Mirror Lake. It keeps the peace that way. Mirror Lake encompasses 27 acres of clear water that harbors brook and rainbow trout. Forty percent of the bank is fishable; if you bring a raft or canoe you can get to that other 60% of shoreline that everyone else misses.

Stream fishers can follow the outlet of Mirror Lake, East Willow Creek. Here, you can catch rainbow, brown, brook, or cutthroat trout. And if you follow East Willow Creek down, you'll come to the big water (and big fish) of Taylor Reservoir. The 2,000-acre lake offers the four fish species described above plus kokanee salmon, lake trout, and pike. There are boat ramps here as well.

If you don't feel like fishing, take a walk. The four-wheel-drive road up to Tincup Pass is a couple of miles to the top and makes a great day hike. If you prefer, tramp a section of the Timberline Trail. The trailhead is a few hundred yards below the campground. This path generally follows the timber line north below the Sawatch Range. You can take the trail just a mile or so to Garden Basin and an old mine site, or you can walk all the way to Sanford Creek.

Mirror Lake may be best suited for getting an attitude adjustment in an alpine setting, a place to reflect on the really important things in life, like watching the sun set from the top of the Rockies.

KEY INFORMATION

Mirror Lake Campground
Gunnison Ranger District
216 North Colorado
Gunnison, CO 81230

Operated by: U.S. Forest Service

Information: (970) 641-0471; www.fs.fed.us/r2/gmug

Open: Mid-June through October

Individual sites: 10

Each site has: Picnic table, fire ring

Site assignment: First come, first served; no reservation

Registration: Self-registration on site

Facilities: Vault toilets (no water)

Parking: At campsites only

Fee: $6 per night

Elevation: 11,000 feet

Restrictions

    Pets—On leash only

    Fires—In fire rings only

    Alcoholic beverages—At campsites only

    Vehicles—16 feet

    Other—14-day stay limit

To get there: From Almont, drive north on FS 742 (Taylor Canyon Road) for 22 miles to Taylor Reservoir. Turn right at sign for Tincup on FS 765, and follow 765 for 8 miles to Tincup. In Tincup, turn left on FS 265 and follow it 3 miles to Mirror Lake.

MUELLER STATE PARK
Woodland Park

Many claim Mueller State Park to have views and scenery in Colorado second only to Rocky Mountain National Park. While this is debatable, it is evident that Mueller is blessed with a panoramic piece of land. Pikes Peak is in full view to the east and a long stretch of the Continental Divide lies in sight to the west. The immediate spruce, fir, and aspen slopes, broken with meadows and rock outcrops, serve as the canvas on which a clean, well-kept campground and a complete network of trails make up Mueller State Park.

The commendable upkeep of quality facilities is immediately noticeable when you arrive at Mueller. While riding the smooth, paved road to the immaculate, well-groomed campground, you'll wish all tenting locales could look this nice. The camping area is set in the high country along Revenuers Ridge, with several roads spurring off the main ridge road. The first spur road is Peak View. Here, five campsites are set in woods that look up to Pikes Peak. These sites are usually dominated by RVs and are among 11 total campsites that are open year-round.

The main campground road, divided into two one-way roads, has campsites all along it, including several pull-through sites. Then, Conifer Ridge splits off to the right. True to its name, spruce, fir, and pine cloak its slopes. All types of campers enjoy this area. Farther up Revenuers Ridge on your

CAMPGROUND RATINGS

Beauty: ★★★★★
Site privacy: ★★★
Site spaciousness: ★★★
Quiet: ★★★
Security: ★★★★★
Cleanliness/upkeep: ★★★★★

Mueller is the ideal place to break into Rocky Mountain tent camping and hiking.

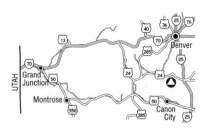

left is Prospectors Ridge. Here is a 12-site walk-in tent camping area. The woods are thick and campsites are strung out far from one another for more than 100 yards. If you want the maximum in solitude and privacy, pitch your tent here.

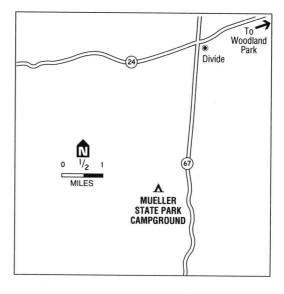

More campsites are laid out along the main road as you continue to Turkey Meadow. The meadow is a ten-site, walk-in tent camping area. Pines and firs shade most of the campsites, except those on the meadow's edge; no matter where you are, the view of Pikes Peak is majestic. Feel fortunate if you get one of these campsites.

The campground ends with more campsites and an auto turnaround on Grouse Mountain. The tent camping areas are the best, but there is not a bad site in this well-designed campground. Water spigots and vault toilets are situated throughout Mueller. The showers, flush toilets, and laundry facilities are centrally located in the Campers Services building.

This campground stays booked from June through August. If you want to stay here—and I highly recommend that you do—come during the week, and make reservations no matter when you camp. It is an ideal starter park for camping novices, and veterans will appreciate the extra special touch the state puts on at Mueller.

The same goes for recreation here. The trails are well marked and maintained. There are over 85 miles of pathways, most open to both bikers and hikers of all skill levels. Some trails are also open to horseback riders. In the backcountry, you can hike to views, open meadows, and old homesteads and mines. There are several ponds in the backcountry for folks to fish. Four-Mile Creek offers stream fishing for trout.

The south end of Mueller has the Four-Mile Day Use Area. This is the trailhead for the popular hike up to Dome Rock. This trek involves several creek crossings. You may see some bighorn sheep from this rock, which rises 800 feet above the valley below.

Park personnel can steer you in the right direction for a trail of your ability. Go to the Visitor Center for answers to questions and also check out the indoor wildlife habitat there. Rangers lead nature programs during the summer in this wildlife-rich park of 12,000 acres. Mueller State Park can get you on your way to being a Rocky Mountain hiking and camping pro.

Also, while you are in the area, make a side trip to the mining town of Cripple Creek and Victor. The historic mining communities have been revamped, offering a little history and a lot of gaming.

> To get there: From Woodland Park, drive west on CO 24 for 7 miles to Divide. Then turn left on CO 67 south for 3.5 miles to Mueller State Park, which will be on your right.

KEY INFORMATION

Mueller State Park Campground
P.O. Box 39
Divide, CO 80814

Operated by: Colorado State Parks

Information: (719) 687-2366; parks.state.co.us/mueller

Open: Main campground mid-May through mid-October; Peak View Loop and six other sites year-round

Individual sites: 22 walk-in tent-only sites, 99 other

Each site has: Tent-only has tent pad, fire grate, picnic table; others also have water and electricity

Site assignment: By advance reservation or pick an available site on arrival

Registration: By phone (call (800) 678-CAMP or (303) 470-1144 in Denver)

Facilities: Hot showers, vault and flush toilets, laundry, phone

Parking: At campsites or walk-in tent camping parking area

Fee: $4 Parks Pass plus $10 per night walk-in tent site, $14 others

Elevation: 9,500 feet

Restrictions

> *Pets*—On leash only, not allowed on trails
>
> *Fires*—In fire grates only
>
> *Alcoholic beverages*—3.2% beer only
>
> *Vehicles*—2 allowed at larger sites
>
> *Other*—14-day stay limit

RUBY MOUNTAIN

Buena Vista

A rushing, frothing torrent of whitewater emanating from the state's highest peaks forms a 150-mile stretch of the Arkansas River that attracts boaters from Colorado and beyond. Here, several public agencies, most notably the Bureau of Land Management (BLM) and Colorado State Parks, have formed the Arkansas Headwaters Recreation Area. Ruby Mountain Campground is right in the heart of the recreation area, where you can not only raft and kayak but also fish and hike.

This campground is a getaway from the bustle of the river corridor. Ruby Mountain will be on your left and the Arkansas River will be on your right as you enter the riverside campground. To your right is a parking area and six campsites that lie at the river's edge. Some of the campsites are shaded by large cottonwoods, others have low willows and other brush that offer little in the way of sun protection. The campsites are a little too close together for my taste, but river-runners grab them up first every time. The rush of the water must give them a pre-boating rush of adrenaline.

A short distance from the water is a small loop with five campsites centered around a bathroom and changing area. One site is streamside, next to the launch area. Two of the campsites are inside the loop by the changing area, and the other two are farther away from the river in the open. The saving grace of these campsites is their recent

CAMPGROUND RATINGS

Beauty: ★★★
Site privacy: ★★
Site spaciousness: ★★★
Quiet: ★★
Security: ★★★
Cleanliness/upkeep: ★★★

Camp directly on Colorado's most popular whitewater river, the Arkansas.

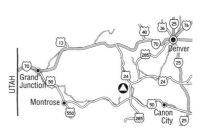

refurbishment, which included new tent pads.

Farther up the hill is a drive with nine campsites overlooking the river. The sites have been leveled and are camper-friendly, with steps accessing the various leveled areas on which picnic tables and tent pads lie. The hill and some piñon pine offer some decent shade, though two of the sites are out in the open. These are the best overall campsites. You'll find two nicely wooded, very private campsites all alone up a small side can-yon on the left a short distance down Chaffee County Road 300.

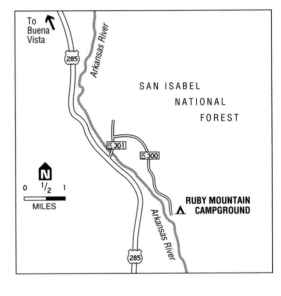

I recommend making reservations at Ruby Mountain during the summer whitewater season. Weekends are obviously busier, but many boaters come from far away, so there's no telling how full the campground will be. You shouldn't have much of a problem getting a site the rest of the year. Also, remember to bring your own water, as none is furnished. If you forget your water, the town of Buena Vista is just a short distance away. Other supplies and rafting companies are there as well.

The Arkansas River drops more than 5,000 feet in the first 120 miles of its journey to meet the Mississippi River. The river flows through rocky canyons, wide-open valleys, and slower sections that appeal to fishermen. Browns Canyon is a highlight of any boating trip. Here, brown granite walls and a ponderosa and piñon-juniper woodland loom overhead. But don't forget to keep your eye on the river while bouncing through the rapids.

The river slows down a bit before entering the Lower Arkansas River Canyon. Here are a series of rough and rugged rapids that have been christened with names like Maytoag, Lose-Your-Lunch, and Shark's Tooth. Then comes the 1,000-foot-high walls of the Royal Gorge and an 8-mile section of rapids as difficult as the scenery is spectacular.

Fishermen visit the river during the lower-water months of March, April, May, September, and October. Getting around on the Arkansas River is a lot easier then, as anglers vie for wild brown and rainbow trout. The Arkansas Headwaters Recreation Area maintains fishing access points along the river. Make sure you are not fishing on any of the private lands intermixed with public land. Commercial float fishing trips are offered by local outfitters.

Just up from the campground is the Browns Canyon Wilderness Study Area. The study area is on the eastern side of the river corridor, in a transition zone where the piñon-juniper forest gives way to the spruce-fir forest of the high country. Just downstream and to the left of the campground is the trail that leads up the Middle Cottonwood Gulch, where you can escape the bustle of the river corridor and enjoy some quiet nature. I recommend making the hike early in the morning while the canyon is still in the shade and the sun shines on the Collegiate Peaks across the valley. Then you can go rafting in the afternoon, when the weather is a little warmer.

To get there: From the Johnson's Village intersection of U.S. 24 and U.S. 285, continue south on U.S. 285 to CR 301. Cross the Arkansas River, heading east on CR 301, and continue until the pavement ends. Turn right on CR 300 and follow it 2.4 miles to Ruby Mountain Campground. Note the 15 m.p.h. speed limit.

KEY INFORMATION

Ruby Mountain Campground Arkansas Headwaters Recreation Area
P.O. Box 126
Salida, CO 81201

Operated by: Colorado State Parks and the Bureau of Land Management

Information: (719) 539-7289; parks.state.co.us/arkansas

Open: Year-round

Individual sites: 22

Each site has: Tent pad, fire grate, picnic table

Site assignment: By reservation or first come, first served

Registration: By phone (call (800) 678-CAMP or (303) 470-1144 in Denver) or online at www.coloradoparks.org.

Facilities: Vault toilets (no water, bring your own)

Parking: At campsites only

Fee: $7 per night plus $2 per person per night

Elevation: 7,600 feet

Restrictions

Pets—On leash only

Fires—In fire grates only; firewood not provided

Alcoholic beverages—At campsites only

Vehicles—30 feet

Other—14-day stay limit

SUPPLY BASIN

Dotsero

The lake-studded White River Plateau is a cool, high-country getaway first used by the native Ute Indians. Now you can come here, stay at Supply Basin, and enjoy the scenery. The rolling meadows here sport more wildflowers than anywhere I've ever seen. These meadows give way to deep gorges bisecting the plateau. Lakes and woodlands diversify the terrain. Views are downright inspiring.

Your first views will come on the drive up from the Colorado River. Coffee Pot Road enters a Gambel oak forest before coming to the highlands, where vast fields overlooking the Eagle and Colorado river valleys are broken by stands of aspen. Stop at the Deep Creek overlook, where a gorge dramatically cuts through the plateau. Then enter lake country, where the wind blows strong and stunts outlying trees. A good wind will keep down flying insects, which can be numerous here at times. Supply Basin itself is a fairly small lake, where spruce and subalpine fir dot the landscape. There are wide views of the Flat Tops and park land around you, as well as nearby Heart Lake.

Climb a small hill, then come to the lake. The first set of sites share a small parking area, from which you make a short walk to a group of campsites, situated about 40 feet above the north shore of Supply Basin. Most of the trees here are undersized from the harsh winters, but they do provide some shade and privacy.

CAMPGROUND RATINGS

Beauty: ★★★★
Site privacy: ★★
Site spaciousness: ★★★★
Quiet: ★★★
Security: ★★★
Cleanliness/upkeep: ★★★

Flowery meadows and alpine lakes await you on the White River Plateau.

98

A short road splits off to the left and features one campsite all by itself. This large site is often used by bigger groups. A second road leads to another isolated campsite that is close to Heart Lake. A vault toilet stands near the entrance to the campground. Be advised there is no water here; you must bring your own or treat the nearby lake water. Broken Rib Spring, located 11 miles back down Coffee Pot Road, is a good source of water (though it also needs to be properly treated

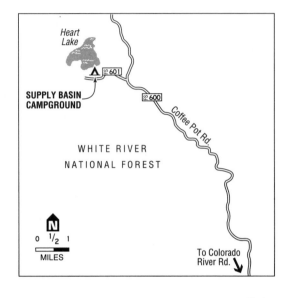

for drinking). Bring all the supplies you may need, for it is a long drive off the plateau and into the lowlands.

Fishing is a natural pastime in an area of so many lakes. These lakes are stocked annually. It is hard for fish to winter up here because the lakes will freeze nearly solid and cut off the oxygen supply for the denizens of the deep. But by the time the campground is open, Colorado Game and Fish will have stocked the lakes.

Just to the north of Supply Basin is 480-acre, island-dotted Heart Lake, where brook trout are stocked. A canoe is helpful here, as fishing from shore is difficult. Enjoy the quiet of the lake; no motors are allowed. Deep Lake has rainbow, brook, and lake trout, which can grow fairly large (Deep Lake holds the state record for lake trout at 36 pounds). White Owl Lake is a much lesser used, 21-acre brook trout fishery. Nearby Bison Lake has no fish.

The surrounding forest land has many hiking trails, but the best area for foot travel is north of Supply Basin in the Flat Tops Wilderness. Head north on Forest Service Road 600 to access this wild area. Drive very carefully if you don't have a high-clearance vehicle. At Indian Camp Pass, take Trail #1816 up to Indian Lake and Shepherd Lake. Shepherd Lake is home to brook trout.

Farther down FS 600 is the South Fork of the White River. This stream has cut a marvelous canyon that pulls you in either direction. To your left, past a private guest ranch, is a wood-enclosed meadow area that leads to South Fork Falls. This waterfall positively roars, especially during the early summer.

Upstream on the South Fork is a large field known as The Meadows. The South Fork meanders through this area and harbors many trout. Trail #1827 continues up the South Fork and accesses other trails to reach the high country. A White River National Forest map is very helpful for exploring this area; buy the map and make the trip. Your visit to Supply Basin will inspire you to return to the Flat Tops summer after summer, just as the Ute Indians did for generations.

KEY INFORMATION

Supply Basin Campground
Eagle Ranger District
P.O. Box 720, 125 W. 5th Street
Eagle, CO 81631

Operated by: U.S. Forest Service

Information: (970) 328-6388; www.wildernet.com

Open: July through September

Individual sites: 7

Each site has: Picnic table, fire grate

Site assignment: First come, first served; no reservation

Registration: Self-registration on site

Facilities: Vault toilet (no water)

Parking: At campsites only

Fee: $6 per night

Elevation: 10,760 feet

Restrictions

Pets—On leash only

Fires—In fire grates only

Alcoholic beverages—At campsites only

Vehicles—25 feet (2 sites only) or less

Other—14-day stay limit

To get there: Head north on Colorado River Road from exit 133 on I-70 near Dotsero and follow it for 1.8 miles to Coffee Pot Road, FS 600. Turn left on Coffee Pot Road and follow it for 28 miles to FS 601. Turn left on FS 601 and follow it 1 mile to Supply Basin Campground, which will be on your left.

WEIR & JOHNSON

Cedaredge

With an average elevation of over 10,000 feet, the Grand Mesa is a cool island of green jutting up from the arid lands of western Colorado. There is a lot of blue up here, too, with over 300 lakes. Several campgrounds to pitch your tent are located up here, but my favorite is Weir & Johnson. To begin with, it is off the beaten path at the end of a side road; this makes for less auto traffic. That's important, because when the snow melts up here, recreationists swarm the mesa like mosquitoes to the scenic lakes. And I don't blame them—once they see how pretty the waters are, rimmed by a spruce-fir forest, punctuated with flowery meadows, they keep coming back year after year. Some come from as far as Tennessee, like the campers I befriended at Weir & Johnson.

This campground also lies between two lakes and has trails leaving the campground to access three more lakes. These lakes are in addition to countless other lakes and the Crag Crest National Scenic Trail that is accessible by auto.

If you have successfully driven to the campground without stopping to wet your fishing line, enter the campground loop. Off to your left are two campsites that are in an area where the Englemann spruce and sub-alpine fir have been thinned a bit. As you continue the loop, the western tip of Weir & Johnson Reservoir is off to your right. A third campsite sits across the road from the lake.

CAMPGROUND RATINGS

Beauty: ★★★
Site privacy: ★★★
Site spaciousness: ★★★
Quiet: ★★★★
Security: ★★★
Cleanliness/upkeep: ★★★

Lakes are plentiful, and the camping is fine here on top of the Grand Mesa.

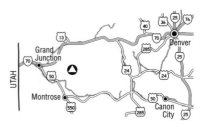

As the loop curves, a small cascade rushes downhill past four excellent tent sites down from the loop road beside Sackett Reservoir. You have to carry your gear a bit to reach them, but you are that much closer to the aquamarine water. The next two sites are also down near Sackett Reservoir. The final three campsites are away from the lake, but are heavily shaded. On my early July visit, one campsite was still too snow-covered to use!

There is a pair of vault toilets for campers. However, the well situation is iffy (currently, a hand-pump is required) and I bet the Forest Service will cap this well eventually. Providing public drinking water is becoming very costly, and there is no fee to camp here to recoup the costs. Bring your own water, and you won't have to take any chances.

You will be taking chances if you try to camp here on July 4 or Labor Day. Weekends can fill, but if you get here by mid–Friday afternoon, you should get a campsite. Campsites are nearly always available during the week.

Trout swim the waters of the two campground reservoirs, and fishing is popular throughout the Grand Mesa, but hike-in lakes often see less fishing pressure. You can walk to Leon Lake. Just cross the Weir & Johnson Dam, hug the shoreline to the right, and cross a small pass to Leon Lake, which is larger than Weir & Johnson. Round Lake and Leon Peak Reservoir are nearby, too. Cross the Weir & Johnson Reservoir dam, then bear left when the trail splits.

After seeing all these lakes, I was wishing for my canoe. Bring yours, or borrow one; you can really get around to less-fished spots on all these lakes up here, nearly 2 miles high. And there is hardly more scenic paddling in the state. If you bring a motorboat, check the regulations—many lakes are too small for motorized craft and don't allow them.

Hiking "the Crag" is tops for foot travel on the Grand Mesa. The Crag Crest National Scenic Trail is a 6.5-mile path that rides the spine of the mesa and offers views in all directions of far-off mountain ranges. On this inspiring hike, you can see all the lakes lying below you like emerald jewels in the forest. The Crag Crest Connector Trail passes through forest and meadow to complete a 10-mile circuit. You can pick up "the Crag" back on Forest Service Road 121 near the Crag Crest Campground, which you passed on the way in.

More information can be obtained at the Grand Mesa Visitor Center at the junction of Colorado 65 and FS 121. Supplies can be purchased at a small store a couple of miles east on FS 121 from the Visitor Center.

KEY INFORMATION

Weir & Johnson Campground
Grand Valley Ranger District
277 Crossroads Boulevard
Grand Junction, CO 81506

Operated by: Recreation Resource Management

Information: (970) 242-8211; www.fs.fed.us/r2/gmug

Open: July through late September

Individual sites: 12

Each site has: Picnic table, fire grate

Site assignment: First come, first served; no reservation

Registration: No registration

Facilities: Vault toilets

Parking: At campsites only

Fee: None

Elevation: 10,500 feet

Restrictions

> *Pets*—On leash only
> *Fires*—In fire grates only
> *Alcoholic beverages*—Allowed
> *Vehicles*—22 feet
> *Other*—14-day stay limit

To get there: From Cedaredge, head north on CO 65 for 15 miles to FS 121. Turn right on FS 121 and follow it for 9 miles to FS 126. Turn right on FS 126 and follow it 3 miles to the dead end at Weir & Johnson Campground.

WESTON PASS

Fairplay

Named after the scenic break in the Mosquito Range, Weston Pass is an often-bypassed campground adjacent to an often-bypassed wilderness. I wonder why, since the neatness, cleanliness, and lack of overuse of the campground were evident immediately upon arrival. One look at the mountains of the Buffalo Peaks Wilderness will make you wonder why you didn't get here sooner. The answer lies partly in what surrounds the area—several other, more popular wildernesses and campgrounds lie between the Buffalo Peaks and the major metropolitan areas of the state.

I prefer smaller campgrounds; they are usually a little more out of the way (read: fewer big rigs) and seem to bring out the neighborliness in your fellow tent campers. Weston Pass has only 14 campsites in an area that I've seen fit twice that many at other campgrounds. The campsites are large and spaced very far apart beneath a forest of lodgepole pine that is supported by other evergreens and a few straggling aspen. The ground cover is mostly smaller trees and assorted rocks and boulders. Landscaping timbers and short concrete posts have been tastefully laid out to keep cars and camping areas distinct. This is part of what gives Weston Pass a certain orderliness not always found at other Forest Service campgrounds.

The South Fork of the South Platte River and a low ridge dividing this creek from

CAMPGROUND RATINGS

Beauty: ★★★
Site privacy: ★★★★
Site spaciousness: ★★★★
Quiet: ★★★★
Security: ★★★
Cleanliness/upkeep: ★★★★★

Weston Pass is one of the nicer Forest Service campgrounds in Colorado.

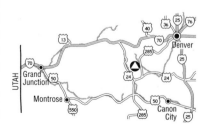

Rich Creek surround the campground. Head along the main drive and admire the size of the campsites set back in the woods several feet from their respective parking areas. Notice the Ridgeview Trail splitting off between two campsites. The seven sites on the main drive give way to a loop road that swings near the South Fork. The loop offers secluded campsites that drop down toward the clearly audible creek. As the loop swings around, one campsite, #11, is actually a walk-in tent site farther up the creek, away from everyone else. A few more of those large campsites are banked against the low, rocky ridge that shades the campground in the late afternoon.

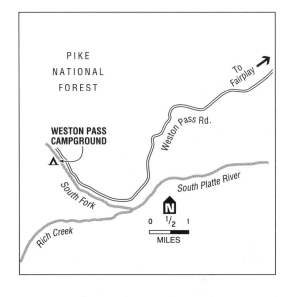

The well is out by the main road just before you bridge the South Fork. Two vault toilets conveniently serve Weston Pass. This quiet campground rarely fills, except on holidays, when you should be avoiding campgrounds anyway.

For your evening leg-stretcher, take the Ridgeview Trail 1 mile to an overlook on the point between the drainages of Rich Creek and South Fork. Take note that this trail also connects you to the Rich Creek Trail, which dives into the heart of the Buffalo Peaks Wilderness. The forests here, from piñon-juniper on the lower western slopes to the bristlecone pines of the highlands, are thick with both trees and wildlife, from bighorn sheep to beaver. This area is decidedly lacking in the human species compared to other wildernesses this close to Denver and Colorado Springs.

One of the better day hikes in the Pike National Forest takes off near Weston Pass Campground. Make an 11-mile loop taking the Rich Creek Trail up to

Buffalo Meadows and picking up the Rough & Tumbling Trail back down. The Buffalo Peaks Wilderness is also an excellent place to build up your peak-bagging skills. Though they are not four-teeners, East and West Buffalo Peak exceed 13,000 feet and have definite tree lines that you pass on the way to sizable rock faces to scale with little difficulty. Take the Rough & Tumbling Trail beyond Buffalo Meadows to the head-waters of Rough & Tumbling Creek, then ascend to the pass where the Rough & Tumbling Trail starts to descend. Veer east first to West Buffalo Peak then East Buffalo Peak. Return to the Rough & Tumbling Trail and backtrack to the campground. This makes a very long day hike, so leave early in the morning for this adventure.

If you don't feel like walking to a view, make the drive up to 11,921-foot Weston Pass. Here, you can look north at a seem-ingly endless range of peaks. You can also stay down low and fish your way around the South Fork or other waters in the wilderness. Or you can enjoy the subtle, relaxing beauty of the Weston Pass Campground. Pass those other places by for a chance to enjoy the Weston Pass area.

KEY INFORMATION

Weston Pass Campground
South Park Ranger District
320 Highway 285
Fairplay, CO 80440
Operated by: U.S. Forest Service
Information: (719) 836-2031; www.fs.fed.us/r2/psicc/sopa
Open: June through September
Individual sites: 14
Each site has: Picnic table, fire grate
Site assignment: First come, first served; no reservation
Registration: Self-registration on site
Facilities: Hand-pump well, vault toilets
Parking: At campsites only
Fee: $9 per night
Elevation: 10,200 feet
Restrictions
Pets—On leash only
Fires—In fire grates only
Alcoholic beverages—At camp-sites only
Vehicles—25 feet
Other—14-day stay limit

To **get there:** From the Ranger Station in Fairplay, drive south on U.S. 285 for 5 miles to CR 5 (Weston Pass Road). Continue on CR 5 until it merges with CR 22 at 7 miles. The campground will be on your left 4 miles ahead on CR 22.

SOUTHWEST
COLORADO

ALVARADO

Westcliff

Alvarado is an active person's campground. On a summer Saturday there will be hikers, bikers, and horseback riders gearing up and heading out on their favorite trails. Several of the trails leave directly from the campground, which is a nice place to return after a day in the scenic Sangre De Cristo Mountains.

Alvarado meets the banner standard set by the Sangre De Cristos. On a slope just into the forest line above the Wet Mountain Valley, Alvarado enjoys a mixture of woodland and meadow, where Douglas fir and ponderosa pines intermingle with aspen. Cottonwood and brush grow thick along Alvarado Creek. Forest density varies with exposure on the three loops. So no matter what your preference for sun or shade, view or privacy, your wishes should be fulfilled, unless it is a weekend holiday, the only time the campground fills.

The first few campsites are in a meadow overlooking the mountains across the valley, then the main road enters a ponderosa grove. The right-hand road, with several nice campsites along it, leads to the Venable trailhead, which is located at the end of this loop. The main campground road continues upward, with campsites on a rocky slope beneath the pines. Another road splits off to the right into a grove of aspen. It has several campsites that offer much shade and some views of Comanche Mountain, high in the Sangre De Cristos

CAMPGROUND RATINGS

Beauty: ★★★★
Site privacy: ★★★★
Site spaciousness: ★★★
Quiet: ★★★
Security: ★★★★
Cleanliness/upkeep: ★★★★

Alvarado is on the eastern slope of the Sangre De Cristo Mountains.

SOUTHWEST

above. The road switch-backs farther up the mountain with more shaded and isolated campsites, then comes to a set of five walk-in, tent-only sites. Here, you park your car and walk a short distance to set up camp. But these sites are on a slope and you may be hard-pressed to find a level place to pitch your tent. However, the entire campground is suitable for tents. This road ends at a turn-around and the Comanche trailhead.

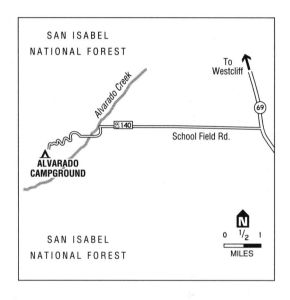

The final set of campsites are on a side road of their own in a ponderosa grove off the main campground road. Water spigots and vault toilets are spread throughout the campground, which is very large to have only 47 campsites. Many of the sites are spread quite far apart. A campground host is stationed at the entrance to the campground for your safety.

Hikers, bikers, and horse riders all enjoy the area trails, most of which lead into the far-flung Sangre De Cristo Wilderness. The Comanche Trail heads up along Alvarado Creek to Comanche Lake. The Venable Trail leads up a couple of miles to Venable Falls, then a few more miles to the Venable Lakes areas. Most of these lakes don't thaw out until late June. You can combine the Comanche and Venable trails and make a strenuous 13-mile loop via Phantom Terrace back to the campground.

If you are looking to stretch your legs but not climb straight uphill, try the Rainbow Trail. It runs 46 miles all the way from south of Alvarado north to Salida. You can use the Rainbow Trail to connect to other trails entering the Sangre De Cristo Wilderness. The Godwin Trail, one watershed north, climbs to alpine lakes. The Cottonwood Trail, one watershed south, climbs along Cottonwood Creek. Any of these bodies of water are suitable for fishing.

You can also drive to within a quarter of a mile of Hermit Lake, another alpine body of water high in the mountains. Take County Road 160 (Hermit Road) west out of Westcliff and drive 13 miles to a signed parking area near the lake. Bring your fishing pole.

You can reward yourself after all that exercise with a good meal at the Alpine Lodge, which is located a few steps from the campground. Or you can drive into Westcliff and take the walking tour of the downtown area. Get your self-guiding brochure at the Tourist Information Center caboose. There is ample food, drink, and supplies here in town, also.

KEY INFORMATION

Alvarado Campground
San Carlos Ranger District
3170 East Main Street
Canon City, CO 81212
Operated by: Rocky Mountain Recreation

Information: (719) 269-8500; www.fs.fed.us/r2/psicc/sopa

Open: June through mid-September

Individual sites: 47

Each site has: Picnic table, fire grate

Site assignment: First come, first served; no reservation

Registration: Self-registration on site

Facilities: Water spigot, vault toilets, trash pick-up, electricty and phone available at host station

Parking: At campsites only

Fee: $10 per night

Elevation: 9,000 feet

Restrictions

Pets—On leash only

Fires—In fire rings only

Alcoholic beverages—At campsites only

Vehicles—35 feet

Other—14-day stay limit

To **get there:** From the courthouse in Westcliff, drive south on CO 69 for 3 miles to CR 140 (School Field Road). Turn right on CR 140 and follow it for 6 miles to Alvarado Campground.

BEAR LAKE

La Veta

Snowy, granite domes of the Sangre De Cristo Mountains plunge down to a forest of spruce and fir. This in turn gives way to an open meadow and Bear Lake, where you can enjoy tent camping, in the most southeasterly slice of national forest land in Colorado. Fishing comes naturally with all the water around, both still and moving. You can move along many trails in the vicinity and make a side trip to the Spanish Peaks, a National Natural Landmark.

The campground is well placed next to the dense forest and mountain meadow above Bear Lake. Along the campground's gravel loop, several wooded campsites are situated to your right with obscured views of Bear Lake. More open sites with occasional stray aspen are in the center of the loop as the road swings around into the grassy meadow. What these campsites lack in privacy they make up in views of Steep Mountain above, the nearby meadow, and a cathedral of peaks beyond. A few campsites on the outside of the loop face into the clearing, which has a stream flowing through it.

The Indian Creek trailhead starts just beyond campsite #9. The loop road begins to climb into the forest again. Another creek rushes from the high country through the campground to Bear Lake. The next few campsites are in the spruce to your right, offering the most in campsite privacy.

CAMPGROUND RATINGS

Beauty: ★★★★
Site privacy: ★★
Site spaciousness: ★★★
Quiet: ★★★★
Security: ★★★★
Cleanliness/upkeep: ★★★★

The magnificent Sangre De Cristo Mountains provide a scenic backdrop for Bear Lake.

SOUTHWEST

This is one of the highest campgrounds around, so bring that extra blanket and expect to find temperatures around, or possibly below, freezing through out the summer. Be prepared for windy, cool conditions any time at Bear Lake. Stake your tent down extra taut as well, because the gusts of wind from the peaks above can blow mighty strong. Cover yourself from the penetrating rays of the sun. Experience taught me these lessons the hard way. On my visit I failed to bring

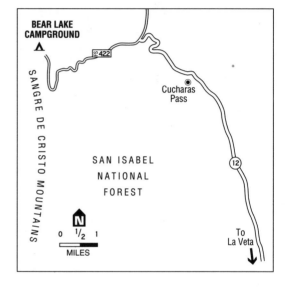

enough clothes for the chill, my face got sunburned, my tent was blown over, and I froze my tail off that night. And I *still* like this place.

Vault toilets are located at the center of the loop and near the Indian Creek trailhead. An old-fashioned pump provides water at the height of the campground. For your safety and security a campground host is situated at the beginning of the loop. Bring your supplies as it is a far piece to the nearest full-service grocery store.

After setting up camp, why not check out Bear Lake? A foot trail circles the deep blue trout-laden water fed by streams from above. Drop in a line or two. No luck? Try Blue Lake. It's a mile by foot or road to the almost equally scenic fishing waters. You'll pass a few other small lakes along the way if you walk. For anglers who prefer moving water try fishing Cucharas Creek. It winds along Forest Service Road 422, your route up to Bear Lake.

Hikers have two nearby options in addition to Bear and Blue Lakes. Take the Indian Creek Trail from the campground north to Bonnet Park or make a loop via Baker and Dodgeton Creeks. Ambitious hikers will want to take the

3.5-mile gut-buster up the old North Fork four-wheel-drive road to Trinchera Peak (13,517 feet). The view will get your heart pumping again. This trek starts near Blue Lake.

Take your camera just south of Bear Lake on Colorado 12 to Cucharas Pass. FS 46 leads from the pass to the Spanish Peaks. These two granite domes are an offshoot of the Sangre De Cristo Mountains and will deliver scenery overload if you head to and beyond 11,000-foot Cordova Pass.

The isolation and long drive with no population base nearby make this a quiet campground, though there may be some site competition on summer holidays. Just come better prepared than I was.

KEY INFORMATION

Bear Lake Campground
San Carlos Ranger District
3170 East Main Street
Canon City, CO 81212
Operated by: U.S. Forest Service
Information: (719) 269-8500; www.fs.fed.us/r2/psicc/sanc
Open: Memorial Day through mid-October
Individual sites: 15
Each site has: Picnic table, fire grate, trash pick-up
Site assignment: First come, first served; no reservation
Registration: Self-registration on site
Facilities: Pump well water, vault toilets
Parking: At campsites only
Fee: $10 per night
Elevation: 10,500 feet
Restrictions
 Pets—On leash only
 Fires—In fire grates only
 Alcoholic beverages—At campsites only
 Vehicles—40-feet
 Other—14-day stay limit

To get there: From La Veta, drive north on CO 12 for 13 miles to FS 422. Turn left on FS 422 and follow it for 5 miles to Bear Lake Campground.

BURRO BRIDGE

Dolores

You've heard the saying before about real estate—the three most important things are location, location, location. Location is indeed the best thing about Burro Bridge. The site of the small campground is the head of a meadow, fringed in woodland on a perch above the West Dolores River. It meets the expectations of high-country beauty you've come to expect in Colorado's national forest campgrounds. However, the nearby Lizard Head Wilderness exceeds the beauty expected from the state's wilderness areas. The state's westernmost fourteener and views of the arid, red rock country to the west are two highlights of this wilderness. And proximity to the Lizard Head makes Burro Bridge a tent camper's choice campground. Tent campers with horses are welcome here, too.

The 15 campsites are strung along a two-way gravel road with a vehicle turnaround at the end. Aspen and spruce are the primary forest components. The understory is grass, flowers, and young aspen. To your left is the meadow and a rising mountain of solid aspen. To your right is the small canyon of the West Dolores River. An attractive log fence borders the campground along the edge of the precipice that drops down into the West Dolores River (the Forest Service doesn't want you to fall into the river on a midnight bathroom run).

The first campsite is nestled in a shade-lending spruce coppice. The next two are

CAMPGROUND RATINGS

Beauty: ★★★
Site privacy: ★★★
Site spaciousness: ★★★★★
Quiet: ★★★★
Security: ★★★
Cleanliness/upkeep: ★★★

Burro Bridge is next to the Lizard Head Wilderness, which encompasses the high peaks of the San Miguel Mountains.

SOUTHWEST

by the canyon, but are more open and each has a shade tree near the picnic table. Farther down, a few sites are away from the river in the sunny meadow. This affords little shade, but good views of the surrounding mountains.

The road climbs gently up along the meadow, passing the vault toilets for each gender, a pump well, and a small horse corral. Campsites continue on both sides of the road, sunny sites on the left and shadier sites on the right. There is a campsite surrounded by young aspen in the middle of the vehicle turnaround.

The last three sites on the outer auto turnaround are beneath a thick stand of spruce and are very shady. The last campsite is set far from the road and is Burro Bridge's most private site. Overall, the meadow sites provide less privacy, and the riverside sites offer more privacy. The large distance between campsites makes privacy less of an issue and abundant site spaciousness the norm.

With so many campgrounds in the area and being farther from the main roads, Burro Bridge receives light use. You may have it all to yourself on a weekday. Weekends may see a few other tent and horse campers, but expect to find a campsite on all but the major summer holidays.

Though it is not the highest peak, the 400-foot spire at its top makes Lizard Head the most conspicuous mountain in the wilderness. It is not scaleable except by expert climbers. There are three fourteeners (Colorado-speak for 14,000-foot or higher mountains) in the Lizard Head. Alpine lakes, waterfalls, and deserted mines complement the high mountains.

Your ticket to all this is the Navajo Lake Trail, which starts a mile above Burro Bridge. The trail crosses the West Dolores, passes two sets of falls, then comes to Navajo Lake. Much of this hiking will be at or above the timber line, so bring clothing for foul weather. A good loop hike uses Navajo Lake Trail then returns to the road above Burro Bridge on the Kilpacker Trail. A little of this hike will be on a forest road.

A good view of the peaks of Lizard Head can be seen while driving over to Colorado 145 to Lizard Head Pass. The historic Rio Grande Southern Railroad wound through this pass. Start a high-country hike from Lizard Head Pass to the spire of Lizard Head on the Lizard Head Trail.

The Calico Trail is also nearby Burro Bridge. Use Forest Service Road 471 to make this 17-mile network of trails any length you like. Mountain bikers should take note of the Stoner Mesa area. This and the Taylor Mesa area offer 150 square miles of high-country forest for hikers, bikers, horse riders, and four-wheel-drive vehicles. Set up camp at Burro Bridge, get out your San Juan National Forest map, and begin exploring.

KEY INFORMATION

Burro Bridge Campground
Mancos-Dolores Ranger District
100 North 6th Street
Dolores, CO 81323
Operated by: U.S. Forest Service
Information: (970) 882-7296; www.wildernet.com
Open: June through September
Individual sites: 15
Each site has: Picnic table, fire ring
Site assignment: First come, first served; no reservation
Registration: Self-registration on site
Facilities: Pump well water, vault toilets, trash pick-up, horse corrals ($5.00/day)
Parking: At campsites only
Fee: $10 per night
Elevation: 9,000 feet
Restrictions
  Pets—On leash only
  Fires—In fire rings only
  Alcoholic beverages—At campsites only
  Vehicles—35 feet
  Other—30-day stay limit

To get there: From Dolores, drive north on CO 145 for 13 miles, then turn left on FS 535 (West Dolores Road). Follow FS 535 for 25 miles to Burro Bridge Campground, which will be on your right.

CATHEDRAL

Del Norte

As you pull into Cathedral Rock and look for a campsite, you begin to wonder why the Forest Service doesn't charge you to camp here. Then you pat your wallet, dismiss the thought, and go about the business of choosing a spot to pitch your tent. And there are plenty of good campsites in this campground, set in a mixed forest of aspen and blue spruce along Embargo Creek. Cathedral Rock and the La Garita Mountains loom over the locale from across the creek.

The 29 campsites are split about evenly on two loops. The left-hand loop is higher up along the creek. In fact, the upper part of this loop lies astride the confluence of Embargo and Cathedral Creeks. A small clearing lies in the lower center of the loop, as campsites are strung along the heavily wooded banks of Embargo Creek. The forest here is so dense that many of the campsites receive almost no sunlight at all. Others are more open as the loop enters a pocket of old aspens. Then the loop turns back downstream and comes to the clearing again. There is a little rock, Englemann spruce, and ground juniper thrown into the forest mix. A hand-pump well lies at the beginning of the loop, and vault toilets are located at each end of the loop for easy access.

The right-hand loop drops down along Embargo Creek. The woods are denser throughout this loop with very few sunny

CAMPGROUND RATINGS

Beauty: ★★★★
Site privacy: ★★★
Site spaciousness: ★★★
Quiet: ★★★★
Security: ★★
Cleanliness/upkeep: ★★★

The camping here is free, quiet, and relaxed.

SOUTHWEST

CATHEDRAL CAMPGROUND

RIO GRANDE NATIONAL FOREST

0   ½   1
MILES

To Del Norte

sites. Judging by the vegetation growing on some of the vehicle pull-in areas on the upper part of the loop, these sites receive very little use. The lower sites along the creek, though, get taken first (and taken they were on my visit). Three of the campsites were occupied by families that had been coming here for years; the trip to Cathedral was a sort of summer pilgrimage for them. They lauded the attributes of Cathedral until they found out it was going to be included in a campground guidebook, then about-faced and made Cathedral sound like a mosquito-infested hole. Well, it is neither heaven nor hell for tent campers, but it is a nice slice of forest in which to relax and escape the trials of modern life. Cathedral is rarely more than half full—usually less than that—and it is very quiet. It fills maybe one or two weekends per season. The woods provide ample privacy, and the sites are average in size. It does have a worn-in look, like an old, comfortable shoe. This shoe will fit most tent campers.

Relaxing and getting away from it all are at the top of the list here. But if you get tent fever, there are some good hiking trails that leave right from the campground, and other trails are nearby. The Cathedral Creek Trail starts near campsite #1 and leads up Cathedral Creek to the Cathedral Rock. In early summer, wildflowers line the trail. Later in the summer you'll be eating strawberries and gooseberries. There are many crossings of the creek, eventually passing a waterfall on the way up to the jagged cliffs of Cathedral Rock.

The Embargo Creek Trail leaves the upper loop and heads toward Mesa Mountain along Embargo Creek. Views open up a few miles from the campground. The Fremont Camp Trail starts up Forest Service Road 640 a short piece above the campground. Here is where explorer John Fremont and his men spent a long and deadly winter.

Both Cathedral and Embargo Creeks, offer quality trout fishing near the campground. Fly fishing is easier below the campground in the lower elevations along Embargo Creek, where the forest is more open. But if you want to go for the big ones, head down to the Rio Grande. Many portions of the river are Colorado gold-medal fishing waters, which are catch-and-release areas, allowing the trout to grow larger. Rafting is also a popular way to enjoy the Rio Grande. The rapids are generally Class II and III. Outfitters are stationed in both South Fork and Del Norte.

KEY INFORMATION

Cathedral Campground
13308 West Highway 160
Del Norte, CO 81132

Operated by: U.S. Forest Service

Information: (719) 657-3321; www.wildernet.com

Open: Memorial Day through Labor Day

Individual sites: 29

Each site has: Picnic table, fire grates

Site assignment: First come, first served; no reservation

Registration: No registration

Facilities: Hand-pump well, vault toilets

Parking: At campsites only

Fee: No fee

Elevation: 9,400 feet

Restrictions

Pets—On leash only

Fires—In fire grates only

Alcoholic beverages—At campsites only

Vehicles—35 feet

Other—14-day stay limit

To get there: From Del Norte, head west on U.S. 160 for 9 miles to Embargo Creek Road. Turn right on Embargo Creek Road and follow the signs for Cathedral Campground 15 miles distant on FS 650 then FS 640. Cathedral Campground will be on your right.

GREAT SAND DUNES NATIONAL MONUMENT, PIÑON FLATS CAMPGROUND

Blanca

It was an incredibly windy day as I headed toward the dunes. Dust and sand were blowing across the San Luis Valley. Blanca Peak towered on my right, somewhat clouded by the airborne grit. Later, the Great Sand Dunes appeared, a massive shifting swath of sand, contrasting with the verdant Sangre De Cristo Mountains in the background. The blustery day made it evident how such a peculiar sight could form in the middle of the Rocky Mountains.

Piñon Flats Campground, located in the Great Sand Dunes National Monument, impressed me as well. It is set in a juniper-pine forest complemented with a sagebrush and grass understory between the dunes and the high country. There are two long, narrow loops, each with a variety of campsites to suit almost anyone. The Dunes Trail and seasonally flowing Garden Creek bisect the Piñon Flats.

Loop A is lower and closer to the dunes. A paved road cuts down on dust. Low stone walls level the ground and define boundaries between the 44 campsites. Large rocks keep cars where they are supposed to be. Some campsites are nestled in piñon thickets, others are more open. But the open campsites offer views of the dunes and mountains. Most sites are spacious. As the loop circles back, campsites drop down from the road toward the dunes. These sunny sites offer incredible views of the sands, but they have a more

CAMPGROUND RATINGS

Beauty: ★★★★
Site privacy: ★★★
Site spaciousness: ★★★
Quiet: ★★★
Security: ★★★★★
Cleanliness/upkeep: ★★★★★

You can't imagine the sight of America's largest sand dunes perched against the Rocky Mountains. Come see it for yourself.

120

SOUTHWEST

worn and dusty appearance to them.

Loop B parallels Loop A, but is situated on higher, more wooded ground. It has 44 campsites as well and a few cottonwoods growing alongside Garden Creek, breaking up the evergreens. Elaborate rock work keeps the natural areas from being trampled and levels the campsites. Just beyond the Little Medano Trailhead is a set of campsites that offers great views of the contrasting sand dunes and mountains.

Each loop has two comfort stations with flush toilets, drinking water, and sinks for washing your dishes. Between Loop A and Loop B is a small campground store that is open between May and September. It offers typical camp supplies, such as ice, wood, and soda. If you run out of something, buy it here; otherwise, I suggest making a major supply run before you get to the dunes.

Piñon Flats can fill on summer weekends. It is a little on the busy side during summer weekdays. However, from September to May, the campground is quiet and most campsites are available. Late spring and early fall are the best times to visit.

Have you ever climbed a 700-foot sand dune? Here's your chance. Take the half-mile Dunes Trail from the campground down to the dunes and start climbing. The loose sand and deceptive distances make it more challenging than it seems. This is one place where your footprints never last for long. Eighteen miles of more foot-friendly trails lace the park. Head north from the campground on the Little Medano Trail 1.2 miles to a cliff overlooking the dunes. The Piñon Flats Trail connects the campground with the Visitor Center.

The Wellington Ditch Trail is an easy hike along an old settler's irrigation flow. The high country awaits you on the Mosca Pass Trail.

In the summer, there are ranger-led walks every day and ranger programs every evening. Keep your camera handy at all times. The ever-changing light and dunes combine to present an evolving landscape as you explore the environment. These are the largest sand dunes in North America. The unexpected setting for them makes the Great Sand Dunes experience an eye-opening reward and very worth the stop.

Outside the park is the short walk to Zapata Falls. It is on public land a few miles south of the monument on Colorado 150. You can extend the hike 3 more miles up to alpine Zapata Lake. Nearby San Luis Lakes State Park offers fishing, boating, and wildlife viewing. Thousands of acres of the Sangre De Cristo Wilderness lie east of the dunes. A primitive road skirts the monument and heads into this vast national forest land.

KEY INFORMATION

Great Sand Dunes National Monument, Piñon Flats Campground
11999 Highway 150
Mosca, CO 81146

Operated by: National Park Service

Information: (719) 378-2312; www.nps.gov/grsa

Open: Year-round

Individual sites: 88

Each site has: Picnic table, fire grate, tent pad

Site assignment: First come, first served; no reservation

Registration: Self-registration on site

Facilities: Water spigots, flush toilets, community sinks

Parking: At campsites only

Fee: $10 per night

Elevation: 8,200 feet

Restrictions

Pets—On leash only

Fires—In fire grates only

Alcoholic beverages—At campsite only

Vehicles—35 feet

Other—6 people maximum per site; 14 day stay limit

To get there: From Blanca, drive west on U.S. 160 for 5.2 miles to CO 150. Turn right on CO 150 and follow it for 16 miles to Great Sand Dunes National Monument.

SOUTHWEST COLORADO

LOST TRAIL
Creede

Sometimes a long drive on a dirt road ends in disappointment, but sometimes you are rewarded for enduring those bumpy, bouncy, dusty rides. In this case, you find Lost Trail Campground. Lost Trail sits in a beautiful valley surrounded on three sides by the San Juans, which form a horseshoe around the headwaters of the Rio Grande, which flow past your tent. Other peaks and crags stand out in bold relief. There are two outstanding hiking areas nearby and two fishing reservoirs close by as well.

The small campground with the big views has only seven campsites spread alongside lower Lost Creek just before its confluence with the Rio Grande. Mostly rock-strewn meadow, Lost Trail has some spruce and aspen that testify to the tough winters up here. The campsites are spread along a rocky road with a vehicle turn-around at the end. Enter the open campground and pass the first campsite on your right. It lies right alongside Lost Trail Creek and has the shade of some spruce. The next site is located in an especially rocky part of the meadow. The next campsites is opposite the creek and is in full-blown open terrain. The views? Simply outstanding. The shade? Nil.

Pass the hand-pump well and the pair of vault toilets for each gender, then come to the auto turnaround. The fifth site is down along the creek far away from the others. If

CAMPGROUND RATINGS

Beauty: ★★★★
Site privacy: ★★★
Site spaciousness: ★★★
Quiet: ★★★★
Security: ★★★
Cleanliness/upkeep: ★★★

Lost Trail is the grandstand of the San Juan Mountains.

SOUTHWEST

you want privacy, stay here. The sixth site is on a rocky knoll in the center of the turnaround. A few aspens offer scant shade. The last site is away from the creek in the meadow and is another site with all view and no shade.

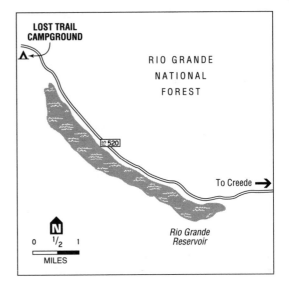

Don't worry too much about privacy—most people who drive this far are going to be like-minded tent campers who want to get way off the beaten track. It's axiomatic: The smaller the campground, the nicer campers are to one another. Come here and you'll probably make some new friends.

If (somehow) you tire of taking in the view from the campground, take a hike. The trail system around here is outstanding. The Lost Creek trailhead is just a bit up the road. Here you can take the Lost Creek Trail up to Heart Lake, or go toward the old mining area up toward the Continental Divide. About 30 minutes up the Lost Creek Trail will find you at the junction with the West Lost Creek Trail. Turn left here and come to a giant landslide caused by avalanche activity in 1991. A lake was formed from this event and the Forest Service has stocked it. (And you thought new lakes were only created by man.)

The Continental Divide Trail is farther up Forest Service Road 520 near Stony Pass. This is the easy way to see the high country. The old Beartown mining site is off FS 520 on FS 506. Just down from the campground is the Ute Creek trailhead. After fording the Rio Grande, you can access the Weminuche Wilderness along Ute Creek. This also makes for an isolated fishing experience.

Two nearby reservoirs also offer fishing. Rio Grande Reservoir is closer, but harder to fish on unless you have a boat. It has over 1,200 surface acres of trout water. Road Canyon Reservoir is a little farther away, however it is much better suited for bank fishing. It has only 140 surface acres, but the shoreline has a gentle grade, parking areas, and spots to put down a chair. The fishing is said to be good.

Bring all you will need to Lost Trail Campground. Supplies are limited in Creede, and you won't have to make an extra trip down that bumpy gravel road.

KEY INFORMATION

Lost Trail Campground
3rd and Creede Avenue
Creede, CO 81130

Operated by: U.S. Forest Service

Information: (719) 658-2556; www.wildernet.com

Open: Memorial Day through Labor Day

Individual sites: 7

Each site has: Picnic table, fire ring

Site assignment: First come, first served; no reservation

Registration: No registration

Facilities: Pump well, vault toilets

Parking: At campsites only

Fee: No fee

Elevation: 9,500 feet

Restrictions

Pets—On leash only

Fires—In fire rings only

Alcoholic beverages—At campsites only

Vehicles—25 feet

Other—14-day stay limit

To get there: From Creede, head west on CO 149 for 20 miles to FS 520 (Rio Grande Reservoir Road) and turn left. Follow FS 520 for 18 miles to Lost Trail Campground, which will be on your left.

MESA VERDE NATIONAL PARK, MOREFIELD CAMPGROUND

Cortez

You've got to see Mesa Verde! The sight of the preserved remains of an extinct culture set into the inherent beauty of this park is one of Colorado's finest natural experiences. While driving on the park entrance road you are thinking about cliff dwellings and ancient cultures, but then you look over the Mancos Valley and San Juan scenery and realize that this place is special. The only extraordinary trait of the Morefield Campground is its size—over 400 campsites. It is a pleasant enough place to stay and has adequate amenities to keep you from leaving the mesa, but the park itself has more than enough attractions to make you want to stay longer—the ranger-led tours, the view-laden hiking, darn good auto touring, and high-quality ranger programs every night.

The plethora of campsites are divided into nine loops and are spread out in a basin surrounded by ridges of trees and stone. In the basin, the primary vegetation is the bushy Gambel oak with some occasional piñon pine. Each loop has comfort stations with flush toilets for each gender and combination water fountains/spigots outside them. A community sink area is also within the comfort station.

Pay your fee at the campground entry station and begin looking for a campsite. On the whole, campsite spaciousness is average; privacy depends on the amount of tree cover, which varies considerably. The

CAMPGROUND RATINGS

Beauty: ★★★
Site privacy: ★★
Site spaciousness: ★★★
Quiet: ★★★
Security: ★★★★★
Cleanliness/upkeep: ★★★★★

You'll need to stay at least one night at the largest single campground in the national park system to see the cliff dwellings and more at Mesa Verde.

SOUTHWEST

forest's understory is generally grassy, with some sections of sage and brush. Navajo Loop is popular with tent campers. It is nestled in a hollow off to your left. The loop has many shaded sites and other sites that are exposed to the full sun, which can be tiresome on a long, summer day.

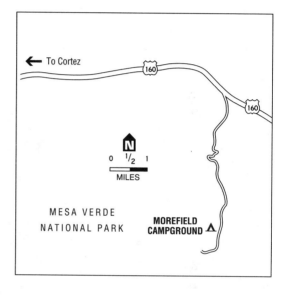

To Cortez

MESA VERDE
NATIONAL PARK

MOREFIELD
CAMPGROUND

0   ½   1
MILES

On down the way, Pueblo Road contains three loops and lots of campsites. This area is on a hill and has some piñon pines. The Zuni Loop is the best loop up here and has many good tent sites with a variety of sun and shade. There are good views across the basin of Prater Ridge.

Stay away from the Ute Loop. It is the only loop with hookups and is the place of choice for RV campers. The Oraibi, Waipi, and Hano loops are all connected to one another. This area has many campsites that take a beating from the sun. The far views are good, but the near views of your fellow campers can be a little too close. The Apache Loop is sometimes closed until the campgrounds begins to fill up. It is similar to the Oraibi loop.

Tent campers share Morefield Campground evenly with RV and pop-up campers. Morefield rarely fills and is fairly quiet, except for summer holidays, especially Memorial Day. A concessionaire offers showers and a laundry for a price. There is also a camp store, gift shop, cafe, and gas station. Snack bars are located at Chapin and Wetherill Mesas. The Far View Lodge, located within the park, offers fine dining. You really can have it all!

Now, the reason why you came—to see the cliff dwellings. You must buy a ticket to go on a ranger-led tour of the three primary dwellings—Long House,

Cliff Palace, and Balcony House. Each one was constructed in the 1200s by the ancestral Pueblos who made their lives atop the "Green Table." Cliff Palace has over 150 rooms. The ranger leading the tours will satisfy your curiosity about each of the sites. You can tour the Spruce Tree House on your own. All-day and half-day concessionaire guided tours of the park leave Far View Lodge and Morefield Campground every morning. Mesa Verde is one place where it is smart to be led around by the nose. You'll want to ask many questions, and these rangers have all the answers.

First check out the park Visitor Center and museum to get oriented after setting up camp. You'll come to the campground miles before the Visitor Center and museum. Make the Chapin Mesa driving tour and see the pit houses that came before the cliff dwellings. View other cliff dwellings from the road. The views of the landscape are exciting, too.

Return to the campground to make the 1.5-mile walk out the Knife Edge to watch the sunset. And for the next day, there is Wetherill Mesa, Prater Ridge, the Cedar Tree Tower, and . . . this place will keep you busy. It is an all-inclusive affair. Bring your camera and a few free days, and have a fulfilling time.

To get there: From Cortez drive east on U.S. 160 for 7.5 miles to the turnoff for Mesa Verde. Turn right and the Morefield Campground is 4 miles on your right.

KEY INFORMATION

Mesa Verde National Park, Morefield Campground
P.O. Box 8
Mesa Verde, CO 81330

Operated by: Aramark Mesa Verde

Information: (970) 529-4475; www.nps.gov/meve

Open: Mid-April through October

Individual sites: 426, some group sites

Each site has: Picnic table, fire grate, tent pads

Site assignment: For reservations call (970) 529-4421 or (800) 449-2288; for group sites call (970) 533-7731

Registration: At campground entry station

Facilities: Water spigots, flush toilets, community dish sinks, phone (showers and laundry for fee from concessionaire)

Parking: At campsites only

Fee: $16 per night, $23 electrical sites

Elevation: 8,100 feet

Restrictions

Pets—On leash only

Fires—In fire grates only

Alcoholic beverages—At campsites only

Vehicles—2 vehicles per site limit

Other—14-day stay limit

MIX LAKE

Antonito

Summer comes late high in the San Juan Mountains. Mix Lake, at 10,000 feet, enjoys the blessings and curses of a short season. It is blessed with light use and a stunning high-country landscape, but the season is short and the weather can be rough. The campground is integrated into the varied topography and vegetation of the land. Mix Lake is scenic itself, but so are other nearby lakes, Platoro Reservoir, and the rugged South San Juan Wilderness.

After you pass the pay station, the gravel campground road begins to switchback upward toward Mix Lake. As you turn, the first three campsites surprisingly appear on your right in a clearing surrounded by young aspen. These sites are fairly close together, but offer good views of the Conejos River valley below. Continue up the mountain and pass campsite #4, all by itself. It has a good view as well as offering the most in solitude. Campsite #5 is perched on a hill with even better views, but is very close to the road.

Then come to the first loop, set in a mixed bag of brush, rocks, grass, and scattered trees. The campground host resides here. The loop enters a dense conifer stand with campsites offering nearly complete shade and privacy. The sites in the center of the loop are more open. These sites and those at the end of the loop avail views of the valley below and the mountains above. Nearly all of the 12 campsites are spread far from one another.

CAMPGROUND RATINGS

Beauty: ★★★
Site privacy: ★★★★
Site spaciousness: ★★★
Quiet: ★★★★
Security: ★★★★
Cleanliness/upkeep: ★★★★

Cool off in the lake country of the San Juan Mountains.

SOUTHWEST

The second loop is the highest and closest to Mix Lake. It also offers just about any combination of sun and shade. There are five campsites here. The two sites closest to the short trail to the lake are the most heavily used. There is a water spigot at the beginning of this loop.

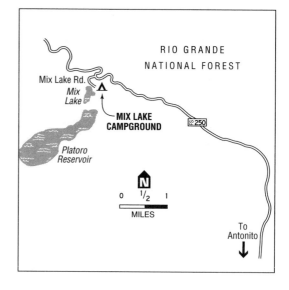

Mother Nature did an excellent job of landscaping this campground. The combination of meadows, boulders, trees, and views will satisfy even the pickiest tent camper. There are three vault toilets in this widespread campground. One is down the hill by the first three campsites; the other two are in the two main loops.

The long drive and nearby private resorts conspire to make this a quiet campground. Expect to find a site on all but the busiest summer weekends. Supplies can be had in the little village of Platoro just a mile down the hill. Expect to be gouged a bit when you buy them.

There are, however, many good things nearby, like Mix Lake itself. A short trail leaving the upper loop will take you to an overlook. Beyond is the massive Conejos Peak. Dark blue Mix Lake sits waiting below, with rainbow trout ready to match wits with you. Just a mile distant is the much larger Platoro Reservoir. This dammed lake is 700 acres in size and offers rainbow and brown trout. Just up toward Stunner Pass are Lily Lake and Kerr Lake. These are accessible from Forest Service Road 257.

There are three convenient trailheads leading into the remote South San Juan Wilderness. The weathering of volcanic rock over the ages by wind, water, and glaciers has left jagged peaks, alpine lakes, and towering forests.

Rugged trails and the lack of 14,000-foot-high mountains keep the crowds away. Two trails enter the wilderness from FS 105. Take Trail #719 for the short, but steep, climb past Tobacco Lake on the way to Conejos Peak, 13,172 feet of rock offering unspoiled views of the wilderness and beyond. After climbing Conejos Peak you'll be glad it wasn't 14,000 feet.

Head up to Bear Lake on Trail #721. Or take a trip to the Three Forks, where the headwaters of the Conejos River come together. This trail, #712, starts beyond Platoros Reservoir. The Continental Divide Trail runs 40 miles through the length of the wilderness.

Below the wilderness, the Conejos River is a popular fishing destination itself. The river scenery has been recommended for wild and scenic designation. It is interspersed with private holdings, so be careful about where you wet your line.

KEY INFORMATION

Mix Lake Campground
Conejos Peak Ranger District
15571 County Road T-5
La Jara, CO 81140

Operated by: U.S. Forest Service

Information: (719) 274-8971; www.wildernet.com

Open: Memorial Day through Labor Day

Individual sites: 22

Each site has: Tent pad, fire ring

Site assignment: First come, first served; no reservation

Registration: At concessionaire

Facilities: Water spigot, vault toilets, trash pick-up

Parking: At campsites only

Fee: $9 per night

Elevation: 10,000 feet

Restrictions

Pets—On leash only

Fires—In fire rings only

Alcoholic beverages—At campsites only

Vehicles—25 feet

Other—14-day stay limit

To get there: From Antonito drive 22 miles west on CO 17 to FS 250. Turn right on FS 250 for 24 miles to the signed left turn for Mix Lake Campground. Follow this road for 1 mile to Mix Lake Campground.

NORTH CRESTONE

Moffat

North Crestone is one of the best camp-grounds in southwestern Colorado. Most other campgrounds are in a wood-land with two or three tree types. Here, along North Crestone Creek, grows an abundance of tree types, especially by Rocky Mountain standards. The camp-ground's location in a forest transition zone along a well-watered valley produces this biodiversity. Cottonwoods, piñon pine, juniper, Douglas fir, maple, alder, and aspen conspire to form a dense forest, where campsites are nestled into nooks and crannies between streamside boulders.

Being in the foothills of the Sangre De Cristo Mountains contributes to making this a desirable place to tent camp. Craggy, barren, snow-covered peaks, alpine lakes, far-reaching views of the San Luis Valley and mountains beyond make the hiking some of the most scenic in the state. The upper reaches of these highlands are pro-tected wilderness.

The campground begins just after you enter the Rio Grande National Forest. On your left is a rocky, tree-studded canyon wall. To your right is the crashing Crestone Creek, shaded by all those wonderful trees. A heavy understory of younger trees and alder screens you from everyone else.

The first set of campsites are set into the woods. The camper parking spots are along the two-way road. At each site, the picnic tables and fire grates are located a

CAMPGROUND RATINGS

Beauty:	★★★★★
Site privacy:	★★★★★
Site spaciousness:	★★★
Quiet:	★★★★
Security:	★★★
Cleanliness/upkeep:	★★★★

North Crestone offers creekside camping in a diverse riparian forest perched against the Sangre De Cristo Mountains.

SOUTHWEST

short walk from the parking spots closer to the creek. A vault toilet and pump well serve these four campsites.

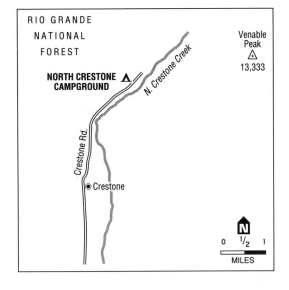

The next set of campsites are farther up the road by a good 100 yards. These campsites are notched into flat areas among the boulders and trees wher-ever they can fit. There are a couple of sites that offer some sun, but expect to be in the shade most of the time in this valley environment.

The final set of two campsites is located just before the end of the road and trailhead parking. One campsite is across the road from the creek—it's the only one that isn't directly next to North Crestone Creek. There is a new vault toilet and pump well up here. A vehicle turnaround and the mountains lie beyond the last campsites.

This is a popular weekend campground, being so beautiful and having so few sites. The upside of having only 13 sites is that even when it's busy, it doesn't seem crowded. But if you want to camp here on a weekend, try to get here on Friday night or early Saturday morning. You won't regret losing a little sleep to camp at North Crestone.

The Sangre De Cristo Wilderness is just a walk away from your tent. The North Crestone Creek Trail leaves the upper end of the campground, heads up, and connects to other trails in the wilderness, enabling trips to the high country. Venable Pass is 5 miles distant, as is North Crestone Lake. The trails here are well marked and maintained. You can fish the creek, which tumbles as waterfalls much of the distance, or North Crestone Lake, where the fishing is said to be good. Wildlife-viewing possibilities include seeing bighorn sheep and bears.

Speaking of bears, they are known to slip into the campground during lean years, so store your food properly.

Campers sometimes walk the mile to the hamlet of Crestone. Here they have a small general store, a tavern, and an eatery. The living is nice and slow here. No tourist traps, just nice people. While you are down there, check out a few more hiking opportunities.

If you take the road past the post office in tiny Crestone and follow it 2 miles up, you will come to the South Crestone and Willow Lake Trails. South Crestone climbs a few miles to South Crestone Lake. The Willow Lake Trail is 3 miles to Willow Lake and Willow Falls. This whole country is very photographer-friendly. I believe the Sangre De Cristos are the most scenic mountains in Colorado. Come here and rate them for yourself.

KEY INFORMATION

North Crestone Campground
Saguache Ranger District
46525 State Highway 114
Saguache, CO 81149

Operated by: U.S. Forest Service

Information: (719) 655-2553; www.wildernet.com

Open: June through October

Individual sites: 13

Each site has: Picnic table, fire ring

Site assignment: First come, first served; no reservation

Registration: Self-registration on site

Facilities: Pump well water, vault toilets, trash pick-up

Parking: At campsites only

Fee: $7 per night

Elevation: 8,300 feet

Restrictions

   Pets—On leash only

   Fires—In fire grates only

   Alcoholic beverages—At camp-sites only

   Vehicles—25 feet

   Other—14-day stay limit

To get there: From Moffat, drive east on CR T (Crestone Road) for 13 miles to the hamlet of Crestone. Follow CR T for 1.2 miles until it turns into FS 950. North Crestone will be on your right.

RIDGWAY STATE PARK

Ridgway

One of the newest Colorado state parks, Ridgway is centered around a 1,000-surface-acre reservoir developed by the Bureau of Reclamation and run by the state of Colorado. This excellently designed recreational area integrates the best in human-made park facilities onto the natural features of the land. Two separate walk-in tent camper areas and three other quality campgrounds make this a must-stop for campers of all stripes.

The Dutch Charlie area features two campgrounds. The Dakota Terraces Campground is on lower, open terrain by the lake and has electrical hookups—this means RVs. The Elk Ridge Campground is high above the lake in a piñon-juniper forest. The views from Elk Ridge of the San Juan and Cimarron mountain ranges will blow your mind. There are two separate loops, both of which have electricity and a surprisingly high number of tent campers. But off Loop D is a set of 10 walk-in tent campsites that will appeal to nearly every tent camper.

Walk the paved path that begins the tent camper loop. The first campsite is handicapped accessible. Beyond that, the gravel path goes beneath some gnarled, old piñons, with separate short paths leading to each well-separated site. Three of the sites are near the edge of a precipice over the lake. The mountain view is like a postcard landscape.

CAMPGROUND RATINGS

Beauty: ★★★★★
Site privacy: ★★★
Site spaciousness: ★★★★
Quiet: ★★★★
Security: ★★★★★
Cleanliness/upkeep: ★★★★★

This is one of the finest state parks in Colorado, if not the country.

SOUTHWEST

All the sites have adequate shade trees, though high noon may present a heat problem. Large, level tent pads make for sound sleeping. Water spigots are located at the tenter parking area. A modern restroom is nearby, though the showers and laundry are in the campers services building 100 or so yards distant.

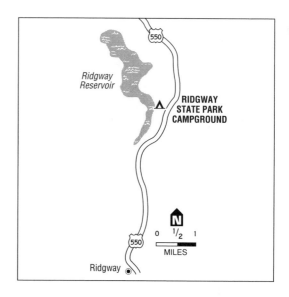

Pa-Co-Chu-Puk Campground, 3.5 miles north of the Dutch Charlie area, has two loops that have water, bathrooms, and electricity, but they are out in the open and full of RVs. However, it also has a 15-site, walk-in tent camping loop that is across the Uncompahgre River from the rest of the park. This loop offers a rustic experience, yet is adjacent to the high-quality facilities that Ridgway offers. This loop is set in a ponderosa pine wood, complemented with Gambel oak and piñon pine, that gently rises up the slope of Log Hill Mesa.

Load your gear on a complimentary cart and bridge the river to the tenters' area. Campsites are snuggled here and there among the trees. The river is clearly audible. At each site, the picnic table and tent pads have been tastefully leveled, making your experience more comfortable, but still part of nature. Most of the sites are on the outside of the loop and are far from one another, making for a private and uncrowded experience. The water spigot is near the parking area and the showers are a good distance away, by the RV loops.

No matter where you are in this park, the first-rate facilities will make you wish all state parks had $22 million to spend on development. Recreating around here is first rate, too. Ridgway Reservoir offers fishing for trout and kokanee salmon. Waterskiing, parasailing, and riding wave runners are popular. No boat? No problem! The full-service marina will rent you anything from a canoe to a pontoon barge. A swimming beach and playground are ideal for family campers.

The Uncompahgre River flows below the reservoir. You can catch and release fish on the river or keep the fish caught on nearby ponds. Hikers have 15 miles of trails that course through the park to tramp. Four miles of trails are paved for inline skaters and bikers. Ranger-led hikes and programs inform campers about the natural resources of Ridgway. Make sure and check out the Visitor Center, too. The Dallas Creek Recreation Site is at the south end of the park. Here, you can hike and fish along the reservoir and also head up Dallas Creek over the pedestrian bridge.

You would think such a fantastic state park would be constantly full. Not so. However, it does get busy around the major holidays and later in the summer. But I have it on the park manager's word that September is the time to visit Ridgway. Be sure to put this gem of a state park on your to do list.

To get there: From Ridgway, drive north on U.S. 550 for 5 miles to the Dutch Charlie entrance of the park, which will be on your left.

KEY INFORMATION

**Ridgway State Park
28555 Highway 550
Ridgway, CO 81432**

Operated by: Colorado State Parks

Information: (970) 626-5822; parks.state.co.us/ridgeway

Open: Whole campground mid-April through September

Individual sites: 25 walk-in tent-only sites, 255 other

Each site has: Tent-only has tent pad, fire grate, grill, picnic table; others also have water and electricity

Site assignment: By advance reservation or pick an available site on arrival

Registration: By phone (call (800) 678-CAMP or (303) 470-1144 in Denver)

Facilities: Hot showers, flush toilets, laundry, phone, vending machines

Parking: At campsites or walk-in tent campers' parking area

Fee: $4 Parks Pass plus $10 per night walk-in tent site, $14–16 others

Elevation: 7,000 feet Elk Ridge, 6,600 feet Pa-co-chu-puk

Restrictions

Pets—On leash only

Fires—In fire rings only

Alcoholic beverages—3.2% beer only

Vehicles—On paved roads only

Other—14-day stay limit

RIO BLANCO

Pagosa Springs

Rio Blanco is one of those small, quiet, out-of-the-way campgrounds ideal for a relaxing interlude with the natural world. Once rejuvenated, you will find plenty of attractions nearby to keep you as busy as you want to be. The Murray Historic Homestead is within walking distance; the wild and little-tramped South San Juan Wilderness is only a few miles away. The town of Pagosa Springs is conveniently close to enjoy the hot springs there or to arrange a rafting trip down the San Juan River. The Ute Indian Reservation offers Indian culture as well.

Rio Blanco Campground is situated on a flat beside the gurgling Rio Blanco River. Pass the picnic area and enter the loop. To your right is a steep hill covered in Douglas fir. A grassy meadow punctuated with large, narrow leaf cottonwoods occupies the center of the loop, as do the first two campsites. Each one is placed near the shade of a cottonwood. These spacious campsites look little used, maybe due to the apparent lack of privacy. But campsite privacy is not much of an issue at this underused campground because each campsite is spread far from its neighbor.

The dirt road loops around where the steep hill meets the Rio Blanco. Here is the third campsite, right by the river, beneath a large ponderosa pine. You can access the river easily after making your way past a fence, which keeps cows from camping with you. The

CAMPGROUND RATINGS

Beauty: ★★★
Site privacy: ★★★★
Site spaciousness: ★★★★★
Quiet: ★★★★★
Security: ★★★
Cleanliness/upkeep: ★★★★

Rio Blanco makes a great base camp to explore the South San Juan Mountains.

SOUTHWEST

fourth campsite is beneath large ponderosa pines, too.

The fifth campsite is the most popular. It drops off the flat down by the river in a grove of fir. You can get sun by the river, yet enjoy shade whenever the sun gets too strong. The sixth campsite is at the end of the loop and enjoys morning shade. It is also by the set of vault toilets for each gender. The pump well is back 200 feet toward the picnic area. It'll give your arm a workout, so be prepared to pump a while before that tasty water comes out.

Don't be surprised if you are the lone camper here. Rio Blanco is not visibly signed from U.S. 84. It should never fill up except on the busiest summer holiday. I stayed with one other group on a Sunday night in mid-June. That same group had Rio Blanco all to themselves the previous Saturday night!

A French Canadian named Provencher thought this area was a fine place as well. He had a homestead and sawmill up the Rio Blanco back in around 1900. But he was flooded out and moved up the hill in 1913. You can follow the old road from the picnic area that leads to the site. Here you'll find the remains of the original barn, a hand-hewn log cabin, and a corral in a meadow with a view deep into the San Juans. The property changed hands over the years until the Forest Service took it over in 1970.

The volcanic rock of the South San Juan Wilderness has eroded into excellent soil and nurtures some of the finest forests in the Rockies. Glaciers have carved deep valleys and ragged peaks, making these mountains ideal for photographers. This wild land harbored the last known grizzly bears in Colorado.

Some believe they may be here still. Don't let that possibility scare you, for there is too much beauty to be seen.

Blanco Basin Road offers good access to the South San Juan Wilderness. From here you can walk the upper reaches of the Rio Blanco. Bring your rod along if you head up Fish Creek or Fish Lake. It's a short walk to Opal Lake, which is named for the milky color of its waters. Fishing for trout is good in the Rio Blanco right from the campground as well.

The V Rock trailhead on Forest Service Road 663 south of Rio Blanco offers access to Buckles Lake, the upper Navajo River basin, and the Spring Creek Lakes. Nearby Eight Mile Mesa is a featured mountain-biking area and sports a lookout tower that offers a view of the Pagosa country.

After all that hiking and biking, you need to relax in a hot spring. Drive into Pagosa Springs and enjoy the naturally hot waters beside the San Juan River at The Springs. Different pools are different temperatures—see how much heat you can take. The mineral-rich springs range from 94° to 111° F.

You can also set up a rafting trip down the San Juan. Outfitters are located all around town. A typical trip will take you down the varied rapids. Other trips offer trout fishing. Pagosa Springs is a western town that hasn't been taken over by big-bucks development and is a pleasure to visit.

To get there: From Pagosa Springs, drive south on U.S. 84 for 10.2 miles to FS 656. You will cross the Rito Blanco and then the Rio Blanco on bridges. After the second river crossing, turn left on FS 656 and follow it 2.5 miles to Rio Blanco Campground.

KEY INFORMATION

Rio Blanco Campground
Pagosa Ranger District
108 Second Street
Pagosa Springs, CO 81147

Operated by: U.S. Forest Service

Information: (970) 264-2268; www.wildernet.com

Open: Mid-May to mid-November

Individual sites: 6

Each site has: Fire ring, picnic table

Site assignment: First come, first served; no reservation

Registration: Self-registration on site

Facilities: Pump well, vault toilets, trash pick-up

Parking: At campsites only

Fee: $8 per night

Elevation: 7,200 feet

Restrictions

Pets—On leash only

Fires—In fire rings only

Alcoholic beverages—At campsites only

Vehicles—35 feet

Other—14-day stay limit

SILVER JACK

Montrose

Silver Jack Campground is arguably one of the prettiest campgrounds in the prettiest spots in the Colorado. Located near the forks of the Cimarron River in the shadow of Uncompahgre Peak, the campground borders 2-mile-long Silver Jack Reservoir, which enhances the forests, meadows, and summits of the nearby Uncompahgre Wilderness. Only hand-propelled boats are allowed on the reservoir, maintaining peace and quiet to go along with the scenery both in and beyond the campground.

The campground is situated on a knoll above the lake, surrounded by aspens. Their leaves flutter in the wind, emitting a purr and creating an ever-changing mosaic of light on the forest floor. Tall grass forms an unbroken understory that contrasts with the white trunks of the aspen. This is the reason you come tent camping to begin with.

Silver Jack has three tiered loops. The roads are paved, along with each camper's parking spot, which really cuts down on the dust. The first loop, Ouray, has a short two-way road with campsites along it before the actual loop starts. Ouray is at the lowest level and has 20 campsites set in the aspens. One small meadow breaks up the trees, along with a very occasional small evergreen.

The Chipeta Loop circles around a meadow of its own. Yet all the campsites are in an extremely dense aspen wood. The young trees make for shady campsites

CAMPGROUND RATINGS

Beauty:	★★★★★
Site privacy:	★★★★
Site spaciousness:	★★★
Quiet:	★★★★
Security:	★★★★
Cleanliness/upkeep:	★★★★★

Stay among the aspens at the Uncompahgre National Forest's finest campground.

SOUTHWEST

and offer great privacy, especially on the upper section of this loop. This seems to be the most popular place to camp.

The Sapinero Loop is the highest on the knoll and is sometimes closed until the campground fills. However, it is my favorite loop. Here, the aspens are older, larger, and allow more light to form a more flowery understory. You can also see the surrounding mountains better. The road rolls upward with campsites spread far apart, though they tighten up as the loop is completed.

Water spigots and vault toilets are evenly spread about the campground. There should be no trouble finding a campsite in June, when the weather is less predictable and can still be chilly. But in July and August, arrive early to ensure a campsite on weekends. September is a great time to visit and watch the aspen leaves change color. Any time is a great time to relax in this wonderful campground setting.

Of course, you may want to get active. Hiking, fishing, and boating are the main activities here. An informal trail circles Silver Jack Reservoir, so you can bank-fish for rainbow trout, brook trout, and kokanee salmon. By all means, if you have a canoe, bring it. Your arms are the only motor you can use here. The scenery from a boat in the middle of the lake is inspiring. You won't care if you catch fish or not.

Fly fishers like to try their luck on one of the three forks of the Cimarron River, as the waters tumble down from the wilderness above. Beaver Lake lies a mile below Silver Jack and is also popular for fishing. The smaller Fish Creek reservoirs are just a few miles north of Silver Jack on Cimarron Road. No one swims in these chilly lakes.

Silver Jack derived its moniker from the mine of the same name located in the Uncompahgre Wilderness just south of the campground. You can hike up the East Fork Trail (#228) to the old mine site. Always be careful near any mine, closed or open. Beyond the mine site are two waterfalls of the East Fork.

You don't have to go to Europe to climb the Matterhorn. There's one right here in the Uncompahgre Wilderness. Take the Middle Fork Trail (#227) for a challenging day hike to top the 13,590-foot peak. Uncompahgre Peak is a four-teener, but can't be reached in one day from this side of the wilderness.

For an easier hike, go to Cimarron Ridge, across the reservoir. It can be accessed from Trail #222. You'll end up at 10,800-foot Lou Creek Pass, overlooking your camping paradise. Or hike up to High Mesa on the Alpine Trail, which starts near the campground. Or you may just want to hang out and watch the aspens flutter in the wind.

To get there: From Montrose, drive 23 miles east on U.S. 50 to Cimarron Road. Turn right on Cimarron Road and follow it 21 miles to Silver Jack, which will be on your right.

KEY INFORMATION

Silver Jack Campground
Ouray Ranger District
2505 South Townsend
Montrose, CO 81402

Operated by: U.S. Forest Service

Information: (970) 240-5400; www.fs.fed.us/r2/gmug

Open: Memorial Day until the year's first significant snow-fall

Individual sites: 60

Each site has: Picnic table, fire grate

Site assignment: First come, first served; no reservation

Registration: Self-registration on site

Facilities: Water spigots, vault toilets

Parking: At campsites only

Fee: $8 per night

Elevation: 8,900 feet

Restrictions

Pets—On leash only

Fires—In fire grates only

Alcoholic beverages—At camp-sites only

Vehicles—30 feet

Other—14-day stay limit

STONE CELLAR

Saguache

When you cross the Continental Divide at South Pass, Saguache (pronounced sa-watch) Park opens up before you. It is an expanse of rolling, grassy terrain cut with creeks and bordered by massive peaks fringed in forest land. Smaller, lesser-used forest roads splinter off in all directions, beckoning you to see what lies over the next hill. Farther down, along the Middle Fork of Saguache Creek, lies the Stone Cellar Campground. Beyond the campground, open park land rolls on to the La Garita Mountains and the La Garita Wilderness.

The wilderness looks over (La Garita means "the lookout") more meadowlands, as well as old-growth forests and trout-laden streams and lakes. There are over 120,000 acres and 175 miles of trails to enjoy in this seldom visited slice of wild Colorado. The Wheeler Geologic Area is also within the wilderness. Rock spires, pinnacles, domes, and other stone oddities emerge from the earth.

When you drop down to the campground, you will immediately notice a lack of trees. That's only appropriate because the campground is in Saguache Park. It took a few minutes for me to get used to the openness, but I began to appreciate the scenery: Middle Fork flowing out of a meadow from above into a canyon down below, vertical rock walls rising up at the campground, and the views of the distant mountains.

CAMPGROUND RATINGS

Beauty: ★★★★
Site privacy: ★★
Site spaciousness: ★★★★
Quiet: ★★★★
Security: ★★
Cleanliness/upkeep: ★★★

Stone Cellar is in the heart of 15,000-acre Saguache Park, the largest meadowland in the entire national forest system.

144

SOUTHWEST

A wooden stock fence surrounds three of the four campsites here. There is one campsite outside the fence a few yards away, toward the head of the meadow on a forest road. This site must either be for campers who have been bad or for campers who love cows, since livestock graze in Saguache Park.

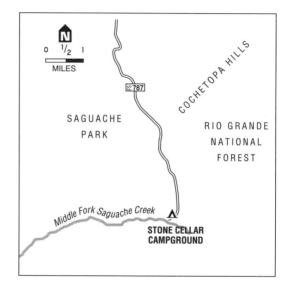

The other three sites border the creek. One site is off to the right and is farthest away from the rock walls. This will avail more views, but less shade. The other two campsites are downstream in a very green, grassy meadow, between a granite wall and the clear, gurgling water. It is a short walk to these campsites from the parking area. A vault toilet and pump well are conveniently set in the middle for all campers, except the site outside the stock fence.

Anyone here should be a tenter, because if it rains, the road back to Highway 114 will be very slick. You shouldn't have a problem unless you are towing something, like a pop-up trailer. If you want to come to Saguache Park but can't stand the thought of camping in the open, several forest roads in the area lead to wooded camp locations. Saguache Park deserves a visit, especially later in the summer when the whole place is awash in wildflowers.

If you do drive the roads around here, make sure to take the marked road to Chimney Rocks. However, to explore the La Garita Wilderness, you must abandon your vehicle and take to your feet. The land is high and the trails start high, then lead even higher.

Farther up Forest Service Road 787 beyond the campground is the South Saguache Trail. It starts at 10,400 feet and follows the creek for good fishing and easy access to the high country toward Half Moon Pass. The Whale Creek Trail starts here, too, and heads toward Palmer Mesa.

FS 744, which turns off right before the campground and has the one lonesome campsite, leads farther up the Middle Fork of Saguache Creek to another trailhead. Here you can walk to the headwaters of the Saguache and into lake country. The Half Moon Pass Trail starts here, too. It is a 7-mile, one-way hike to the Wheeler Geologic Area, but it can be done in a single day. If you leave early in the morning, you will have time to view the area and still return by nightfall.

The North Fork Saguache has its own trail to headwaters made up of several small tributaries; a few beaver ponds are scattered along the way. This trail is outside the wilderness and can be accessed by FS 776. Walk around or drive around, either way you will get an eyeful at Saguache Park.

KEY INFORMATION

Stone Cellar Campground
Saguache Ranger District
46525 State Highway 114
Saguache, CO 81149

Operated by: U.S. Forest Service

Information: (719) 655-2553; www.wildernet.com

Open: June through October

Individual sites: 4

Each site has: Picnic table, fire ring

Site assignment: First come, first served; no reservation

Registration: No registration

Facilities: Pump well water, vault toilets

Parking: At campsites only

Fee: No fee, but donations welcome

Elevation: 9,500 feet

Restrictions

Pets—On leash only

Fires—In fire rings only

Alcoholic beverages—At campsites only

Vehicles—25 feet

Other—14-day stay limit

To get there: From Saguache, head west on CO 114 and follow it 22 miles to FS 804 (Archuleta Creek Road). Turn left on FS 804 and follow it 4 miles to CR NN14. Turn left on the CR NN14 and follow it for 0.8 mile to FS 787. Turn right on FS 787 and follow it 13 miles to Stone Cellar Campground.

TRANSFER PARK

Durango

Transfer Park is steeped in history. The attractive, mountain-rimmed meadow was once a point where tools and supplies were transferred from horse-drawn wagons to mules for use beyond the rugged Florida River canyon in the late 1800s. Ore, mostly gold and silver, would be brought down in the wagons. These days, the 11-acre site is such a scenic campground that it just may prevent you from enjoying the hiking, fishing, rafting, train riding, and town touring that the area has to offer.

Drop into the upper meadow and come to the campground. Miller Mountain stands guard over Transfer Park. There are two camping loops. The right-hand loop has ten campsites and is set in a mature aspen grove mixed with some Ponderosa pine, Douglas fir, and small clearings. Smaller trees and brush form a fairly thick understory. The campsites are large and well separated from one another. Wooden posts delineate each site from one another. The forest closes near the meadow, then opens back up as the loop is completed. You can find just about any combination of sun and shade you desire. There is one vault toilet and one spigot in the center of the loop.

The left-hand loop is lower and closer to the Florida River. Drop down along Transfer Park and the 15 campsites begin. The forest here is more mixed conifers and thus is shadier. The thicker forest and rock outcrops make for a closed-in, intimate feel-

CAMPGROUND RATINGS

Beauty: ★★★★★
Site privacy: ★★★★
Site spaciousness: ★★★★
Quiet: ★★★★
Security: ★★★
Cleanliness/upkeep: ★★★★

Make a transfer to the most attractive campground in the San Juan National Forest.

SOUTHWEST

ing on this loop. The gush of the Florida River can be heard loud and clear. About half the campsites are on the heavily wooded inside of the loop. A few campsites border the river gorge, but a wood fence prevents campers from falling into the river below. Two vault toilets and two water spigots serve this loop.

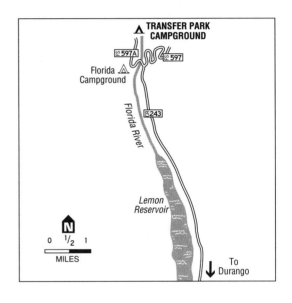

This campground used to be on a reservation basis, but was taken off because it did not fill. Forest Service personnel say it is rarely over 50% capacity. It is an odd fact, but a good one, for tent campers who find their way to this gorgeous place.

Those who do make it here now have to choose among the array of nearby activities. You can trace the old mine trail up along the Florida River. It is primarily used now by fishermen who vie for native cutthroat trout and a few kokanee salmon, which make their way up from Lemon Reservoir. Hiking comes naturally, as the Burnt Timber Trail starts at the top of the campground. This path leads into the nearly 500,000-acre Weminuche Wilderness. A reasonable destination is the southern end of Lime Mesa.

Just up bumpy Forest Service Road 597, which starts by Florida Campground, are two short hikes into Lost Lake and Stump Lake. Lost Lake has no fish. A longer trek goes up Endlich Mesa to the City Reservoir area, which is more attractive than it sounds. Downstream from Transfer Park is Lemon Reservoir. It is a rainbow trout, kokanee salmon, and pike fishery. The popular angling areas are near the dam and at the Lemon Day Use Area.

The rest of the action is down Durango way. It is a historic western town that is cashing in on the tourism craze. The historic district is real, and you can find anything you desire to consume or own. However, if you want to move through some good natural scenery, try the narrow-gauge Silverton Train or a rafting trip on the Piedre or Animas Rivers.

The Durango and Silverton Railroad was constructed in the 1880s to haul gold and silver from the San Juan Mountains. The train trip is an easy way to see the Weminuche Wilderness. It is an all-day affair getting to and from Silverton, but it will be one of the more scenic trips of your life.

The rivers offer more rollicking action. The lower Animas goes through Durango and is a little on the tame side. But the Upper Animas offers Class IV–V rapids. The Piedre has Class III–IV rapids and a wild atmosphere. Contact one of the many outfitters listed at the Durango Chamber of Commerce.

KEY INFORMATION

**Transfer Park
Columbine East Ranger District
367 South Pearl Street
Bayfield, CO 81122**

Operated by: U.S. Forest Service

Information: (970) 884-2512; www.fs.fed.us/r2/sanjaun

Open: Mid-May through Labor Day

Individual sites: 25

Each site has: Picnic table, fire grate

Site assignment: First come, first served; no reservation

Registration: Self-registration on site

Facilities: Water spigot, vault toilets, trash pick-up

Parking: At campsites only

Fee: $10 per night

Elevation: 8,600 feet

Restrictions

Pets—On leash only

Fires—In fire grates only

Alcoholic beverages—At campsites only

Vehicles—35 feet

Other—14-day stay limit

To get there: From Durango, take CR 240 (Florida Road) north for 14 miles to CR 243. Stay left on CR 243, going for 5 miles, passing Lemon Reservoir, and come to FS 597A. Turn left on FS 597A and veer left again after crossing the Florida River. Stay right while passing through Florida Campground and come to Transfer Park in 1 mile.

TRUJILLO MEADOWS

Antonito

Trujillo Meadows exudes a high-mountain aura from its perch near Cumbres Pass and the New Mexico state line. Thick stands of conifers yield to open clearings of grass where cool breezes make summer wildflowers sway back and forth against the backdrop of the San Juan Mountains. The campground is spread wide over the montane setting, standing at 10,000 feet, making the 50-site getaway a much more intimate spot. Trujillo Meadows Reservoir is an attractive mountain impoundment that anglers and canoers can enjoy. The historic Cumbres and Toltec Railroad chugs through Cumbres Pass, offering scenic tours between Chama, New Mexico, and Antonito, Colorado. Possibly the most remote and rugged wilderness in Colorado, the South San Juan Wilderness, is only a few miles away. Here, hikers have an opportunity to get back to the Colorado that the Indians knew.

Leave the well-maintained Forest Service Road 118 and enter Trujillo Meadows. Pass the campground host, located at the entrance for your safety. The upper loop, starting with campsite #1, is much more open. The campsites are set among forest and meadow, giving campers many site, shade, and privacy options. A sunny site may be a good choice on a cool, early summer day.

The second loop, starting with campsite #16, has many tent camping sites, but also

CAMPGROUND RATINGS

Beauty: ★★★★
Site privacy: ★★★★
Site spaciousness: ★★★★
Quiet: ★★★
Security: ★★★★★
Cleanliness/upkeep: ★★★★

This is one of the more scenic and well-kept campgrounds in the Rio Grande National Forest, with much to see and do nearby.

NEW MEXICO

SOUTHWEST

has pull-through campsites that will attract the big rigs. Whoever camps here will enjoy good mountain views, as much of this campsite is in open meadowland with only occasional tree cover. Another small loop spurs off this loop but is often closed unless the campground is full.

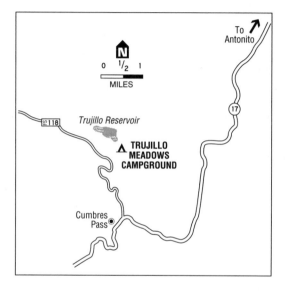

Keep forward and enter the lower portion of the campground. Here you will find campsites #25–49 in an ultradense spruce and fir woodland, which gives off those evergreen aromas that I associate with the high country. This loop slopes off toward a small canyon lying off to the right. The campsites here are fairly close together, but the crowded forest eliminates privacy issues, actually making this the best loop for privacy.

Save your walking for the wilderness trails here, as bathrooms and water spigots are spread evenly throughout the campground. Expect Trujillo Meadows to fill on holidays and weekends in the later summer. Get your supplies in the surrounding lowlands; stores are very scarce in the San Juans.

Trujillo Meadow Reservoir lies just a short distance from the campground. Anglers can cast their line for trout. If you bring a boat, keep your large motors home, this reservoir is wakeless. A canoe would be a better watercraft choice.

Hikers need trails to walk! And the South San Juan Wilderness is as wild as Colorado gets and has over 180 miles of trails to tramp. The last known grizzly bear in the state was killed here in 1979; many folks think if there are grizzlies left anywhere in Colorado, it will be here in the South San Juans. This place is rugged. Pick up the Continental Divide Trail at Cumbres Pass and head north into the South San Juan Wilderness. For closer wilderness access, take FS 1C to the upper Los Pinos River trailhead (you passed it on FS 118 to the campground). Take Trail #736 and enter an alpine land of jagged mountains and sparkling lakes. Other trails spur off Colorado 7 on the way up from Antonito. Take Trail #733 up to Red Lake.

For a less sweaty way to see the scenery, take the Cumbres and Toltec Scenic Railroad. Ride in an open-air car, pulled by a coal-burning locomotive, and get an eyeful of mountainous border country. It was originally built in the 1870s to access the mining fields of the Silverton area. The Cumbres and Toltec Railroad is now listed on the National Register of Historic Places. So climb aboard, and let those old-time engines do all the work.

KEY INFORMATION

Trujillo Meadows Campground
Conejos Peak Ranger District
15571 County Road T-5
La Jara, CO 81140

Operated by: U.S. Forest Service

Information: (719) 274-8971; www.wildernet.com

Open: Memorial Day through Labor Day

Individual sites: 50

Each site has: Picnic table, fire grate

Site assignment: First come, first served; no reservation

Registration: At concessionaire

Facilities: Water spigots, vault toilet

Parking: At campsites only

Fee: $11 per night

Elevation: 10,100 feet

Restrictions
  Pets—On leash only
  Fires—In fire grates only
  Alcoholic beverages—At campsites only
  Vehicles—25 feet
  Other—14-day stay limit

To get there: From Antonito drive 37 miles west on CO 17 to FS 118. Turn right on FS 118 and follow it 2 miles to Trujillo Meadows Campground, which will be on your right.

THE PRAIRIE

BONNY LAKE

Burlington

Bonny Lake is the lowest and most easterly campground in this entire guidebook. Located in a wide valley of the South Fork of the Republican River near the Kansas border, this 1,900-acre reservoir was originally built by the U.S. Bureau of Reclamation in the 1950s. The state of Colorado transformed it into a state park in the 1970s. Now you can boat, swim, and fish in this surprisingly scenic slice of the prairie. The East Beach is the best in tent camping among a good group of campgrounds that circle the lake. If you are coming from out of state, stop here on your way to or from the mountains. You will realize that Colorado really is beautiful all over.

Starting on the northwest side of Bonny Lake is Foster Grove Campground. Cottonwood and willow shade the grassy flat of the campsites, though there is very little undergrowth and thus very little campsite privacy. However, the campsites are spread apart, making lack of privacy less of an issue. The lake is visible, but it is about a half-mile distant. Foster Grove is the second most developed campground here. It has showers and flush toilets.

North Cove is on a small arm of the lake. The campground is smaller, but more popular than Foster Grove. Ten of the 21 campsites face the lake. The sites away from the lake have metal shade shelters over the picnic tables. Although there is no electricity, bigger rigs still dominate this campground.

CAMPGROUND RATINGS

Beauty: ★★★★
Site privacy: ★★★
Site spaciousness: ★★★
Quiet: ★★★★
Security: ★★★★
Cleanliness/upkeep: ★★★★★

Bonny Lake is your prairie getaway in the state's far east.

THE PRAIRIE

There are vault toilets and water spigots, too. A boat ramp and small dock is at one end of the campground with a horseshoe pit nearby.

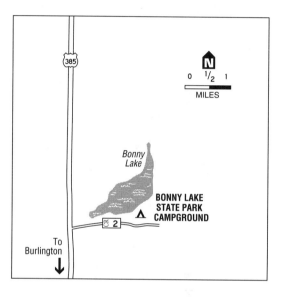

The East Beach Campground is at the southeastern corner of the reservoir near the dam. Drive in and pass three sunny campsites near the lake—they are screened from a view of the beach area by a line of cottonwoods. Under this line of cottonwoods lies the park's best campsites. This is a row of 10 walk-in tent sites, which are by the lake under the trees and have a view of the beautiful waters. Try to get these campsites. Farther on are 20 more campsites exposed to the extremes of the prairie. Thankfully, they do have shade shelters. The lake dam stands tall to your right.

On the southern shore of Bonny Lake near the main body of park development is Wagon Wheel Campground. It has all the amenities including laundry facilities, a dump station, and electricity—this means RVs. Stay away from this campground. A boat launch and marina are nearby.

This is but one of three boat launches scattered around this reservoir with the blue waters. Waterskiing is very popular here, but skiers must make their wakes in designated areas only. You can rent small fishing boats and pontoons at the marina here, and if you already have a boat, storage facilities are available as well. Limited supplies are available here, but I suggest loading up in Burlington.

Bonny Lake is known as one of the best warm-water fisheries in Colorado. Wipers, walleye, pike, bass, and bluegill can be caught in season. Call ahead to the state park for the latest fishing report. Beach lovers don't have to leave land-locked Colorado to get a little sand between their toes. Bonny Lake has several beach areas. West Beach is also a designated swimming area. The other designated swimming beach is near the marina. Other beach areas are not designated for swimming.

Bring a bike and pedal around the lake. The view of the waters and the prairie from the dam is vivid. Bonny Lake is not just for summer. Wildlife viewing is a year-round pastime here. Bird life is particularly abundant. Hunting is allowed in season. No matter what time of year, you will be pleasantly surprised at Bonny Lake.

To get there: From Burlington, drive north on U.S. 385 for 23 miles to CR 2. Turn right on CR 2 and follow it 1.5 miles to Bonny Lake State Park.

KEY INFORMATION

Bonny Lake State Park
30010 County Road 3
Idalia, CO 80735

Operated by: Colorado State Parks

Information: (970) 354-7306; parks.state.co.us/bonny

Open: Year-round

Individual sites: 10 walk-in tent sites, 190 other

Each site has: Walk-in tent sites have picnic table and stand-up grill; others also have electricity

Site assignment: By advance reservation or pick an available site on arrival

Registration: By phone (call (800) 678-CAMP or (303) 470-1144 in Denver)

Facilities: Coin-operated hot showers, flush and vault toilets, laundry, phone, vending machines

Parking: At campsites or walk-in tent campers parking area

Fee: $4 Parks Pass plus $10 North Cove, East Beach; $10 Foster Grove, $14 electric sites

Elevation: 3,700 feet

Restrictions

Pets—On leash only

Fires—In fire grates only

Alcoholic beverages—3.2% beer only

Vehicles—Designated roads only

Other—14-day stay limit in 30-day period

JACKSON LAKE

Fort Morgan

Jackson Lake is an important feature of the northern Colorado high plains landscape. Local farmers depend on its water to irrigate their lands. But before these waters grace the fields, they provide scenic recreational opportunities to all who are lucky enough to come this way. The Rocky Mountains will always be a draw, but this relaxing state park should not be overlooked. Campers can stay overnight in a slew of shoreline campsites while boating, sailing, swimming, and fishing on the 2,700-acre lake. A walk-in tent camping area and lakeside beaches make this oasis even more appealing.

Several campgrounds border the impoundment along the west shore. The Lakeside Campground has wide-open, sun-whipped campsites farther from the lake, but nearer to the water, cottonwoods shade the preferred lakeside sites. A camper services building and shadier campsites are closer to the lake. Then a set of walk-in tent sites stretches along the shoreline. These are the best sites in the park for tent campers. A beach swimming area is near these walk-in tent sites.

The Cove Campground is more open. It has electrical hookups and caters more to RVs. The campsite picnic tables are shaded with interesting shelters that look like the shell of a turtle turned sideways. There is access to the swim beach here as well. The Pelican Campground also has four walk-in

CAMPGROUND RATINGS

Beauty: ★★★
Site privacy: ★★★
Site spaciousness: ★★★★★
Quiet: ★★★
Security: ★★★★★
Cleanliness/upkeep: ★★★★★

Enjoy shoreline camping on this high plains reservoir.

THE PRAIRIE

tent sites a slight distance from the shore and some shady shoreline drive-up campsites. Many of the others are more exposed to the elements. Boaters will want to take advantage of the quick access to the Shoreline Marina and boat ramp just north of the Pelican Campground.

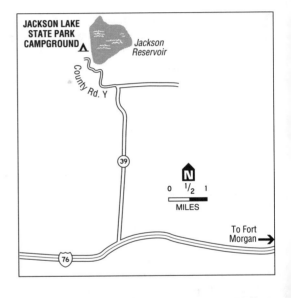

The next campground, Sandpiper, lies on an open slope with numerous planted trees. The height of the hill allows for a great view of the lake, but at the expense of shade and privacy. There is a campers services building and electrical hookups here. Fox Hills is on a wide slope that offers views of the prairie and lake, which is fairly distant. There are many trees here. The final campground on the west shore, Northview, is on an open slope, but has electrical hookups and shade shelters for the campsite picnic tables. These last three campgrounds should be your last choice.

There is one small campground, Dunes, on the south shore of Jackson Lake. This campground abuts some wooded dunes that separate you from the lake, but the water is just a short climb over the dunes. The campground has picnic shelters, but also Russian olive and cottonwood trees for shade. These are more popular sites, and the small size of this campground makes for a quiet camping experience.

Water sports dominate the activities at Jackson Lake. Jet skiing, power boating, and waterskiing are enjoyed during summer months. The Shoreline Marina has limited supplies and most anything a boater might need, including boats themselves, from jet skis to pontoon barges. The west and south shores are designated as wakeless areas. In these areas are two lakeside beaches where swimmers cool off in the waters and sunbathers soak up some rays on the sand.

Bank fishing is popular in the Dike Fishing Area, where boats are prohibited. Both warm- and cold-water species inhabit the reservoir. Trout, walleye, wiper, perch, and crappie are angled for from the Dike Fishing Area and throughout the lake on boats. Anglers who go ice fishing on Jackson Lake increase each winter.

Landlubbers will be seen bicycling on the park roads. Campers can enjoy interpretive programs on summer weekends. You may learn about Jackson Lake's wildlife, especially the wealth of waterfowl. Whether on land or water, you will come away from this pride of the prairie with a new perspective on Colorado.

To get there: From Fort Morgan, head west on I-76 for 14 miles to exit 66 and CO 39. Head north on CO 39 and follow it for 7.3 miles to CR Y5. Turn left on CR Y5 and follow it 2.5 miles to Jackson Lake State Park.

KEY INFORMATION

Jackson Lake State Park
26363 County Road 3
Orchard, CO 80649

Operated by: Colorado State Parks

Information: (970) 645-2551; parks.state.co.us/jackson

Open: Year-round

Individual sites: 262

Each site has: Picnic table, fire ring

Site assignment: By advance reservation or pick an available site upon arrival

Registration: By phone (call (800) 678-CAMP or (303) 470-1144 in Denver), at entrance station or park office

Facilities: Hot showers, flush and vault toilets, laundry facilities, phone, electricity

Parking: At campsites or walk-in tent campers parking area

Fee: $4 Parks Pass plus $9 nonelectric sites, $12 electric sites

Elevation: 4,440 feet

Restrictions

Pets—On leash only

Fires—In fire grates only

Alcoholic beverages—3.2% beer only

Vehicles—None

Other—14-day stay limit in a 30-day period

APPENDICES

APPENDIX A
Camping Equipment Checklist

Except for the large and bulky items on this list, I keep a plastic storage container full of the essentials of car camping so that they're ready to go when I am. I make a last-minute check of the inventory, resupply anything that's low or missing, and away I go!

Cooking Utensils
Bottle opener
Bottles of salt, pepper, spices, sugar,
    cooking oil, and maple syrup in
    waterproof, spillproof containers
Can opener
Corkscrew
Cups, plastic or tin
Dish soap (biodegradable), sponge,
    and towel
Flatware
Food of your choice
Frying pan
Fuel for stove
Matches in waterproof container
Plates
Pocketknife
Pot with lid
Spatula
Stove
Tin foil
Wooden spoon

First Aid Kit
Band-Aids
First aid cream
Gauze pads
Ibuprofen or aspirin
Insect repellent
Moleskin
Snakebite kit
Sunscreen/Chap Stick
Tape, waterproof adhesive

Sleeping Gear
Pillow
Sleeping bag
Sleeping pad, inflatable or insulated
Tent with ground tarp and rainfly

Miscellaneous
Bath soap (biodegradable), washcloth,
    and towel
Camp chair
Candles
Cooler
Deck of cards
Fire starter
Flashlight with fresh batteries
Foul-weather clothing
Lantern
Maps (road, topographic, trail, etc.)
Paper towels
Plastic zip-top bags
Sunglasses
Toilet paper
Water bottle

Optional
Barbecue grill
Binoculars
Canoe with paddles
Field guides on bird, plant, and
    wildlife identification
Fishing rod and tackle

APPENDIX B
Information

Arapaho National Forest
240 West Prospect Road
Fort Collins, CO 80526
(970) 498-2770
www.fs.fed.us/r2/arnf

Bureau of Land Management
2850 Youngfield Street
Lakewood, CO 80215-7076
(303) 239-3700
www.blm.co.gov

Colorado State Parks
1313 Sherman Street, Room 618
Denver, CO 80203
(303) 866-3437
www.parks.state.co.us

Grand Mesa, Uncompahgre, and Gunnison National Forests
2250 Highway 50
Delta, CO 81416-8723
(970) 874-6600
www.fs.fed.us/r2/gmug

Medicine Bow-Routt National Forests
2468 Jackson Street
Laramie, WY 82070-6535
(307) 745-2300
wwwfs.fed.us/r2/mbr

National Park Service
Intermountain Region
12795 Alameda Parkway
Denver, CO 80225
(303) 969-2500
www.nps.gov

Pike and San Isabel National Forests
1920 Valley Drive
Pueblo, CO 81008
(719) 545-8737
www.fs.fed.us/r2/psicc

Rio Grande National Forests
1803 West Highway 160
Monte Vista, CO 81144
(719) 852-5941
www.fs.fed.us/r2/riogrande

San Juan National Forest
15 Burnett Court
Durango, CO 81301
(970) 247-4874
www.fs.fed.us/r2/sanjuan

White River National Forest
9th & Grand, P.O. Box 948
Glenwood Springs, CO 81602
(303) 945-2521
www.fs.fed.us/r2/whiteriver

APPENDIX C
Suggested Reading and Reference

100 Hikes in Colorado. Warren, Scott S. Mountaineers Books, 1995.

Adventuring in the Rockies. Schmidt, Jeremy. Sierra Club Books, 1997.

Along the Colorado Trail. Fielder, John and Fayhee, John. Westcliffe Publishing, 1992.

Backpacking: Essential Skills to Advanced Techniques. Logue, Victoria. Menasha Ridge Press, 2000.

Colorado's Best Wildflower Hikes: The Front Range. Irwin, Pamela and David. Westcliffe Publishing, 1998.

Colorado Nature Almanac: A Month-By-Month Guide to the State's Wildlife and Wild Places. Jones, Stephen R., et al. Pruett Publishing, 1998.

Flyfisher's Guide to Colorado. Bartholomew, Mary and Reynolds, Barry. Wilderness Adventures Press, 1998.

Gem Trails of Colorado. Mitchell, James R. Gembooks, 1997.

A Hiking and Camping Guide to the Flat Tops Wilderness Area. Marlowe, Al. Fred Pruett, 1998.

I n d e x

ABOUT THE AUTHOR

A native Tennessean, Johnny Molloy was born in Memphis and moved to Knoxville in 1980 to attend the University of Tennessee. It was there, on a backpacking foray into the Great Smoky Mountains National Park (GSMNP), that he developed a love of the natural world—a love that has become the primary focus of his life.

Though a disaster, that trip unleashed a passion for the outdoors that has encompassed more than 1,200 nights in the wild over the past 12 years. He has spent over 650 nights in the Smokies alone, cultivating his woodsmanship and expertise on those lofty mountains. He has completed his sixth year as a GSMNP adopt-a-trail volunteer and currently maintains the Little Bottoms Trail.

After graduating from the University of Tennessee in 1987 and continuing to spend ever-increasing time in natural places, he became more skilled in a variety of environments. Upon suggestion and encouragement from friends, he began to parlay his skill into an occupation. The results of his efforts are several books: *Day & Overnight Hikes in the Great Smoky Mountains National Park* (Menasha Ridge Press, 2001); *Trial by Trail: Backpacking in the Smoky Mountains* (University of Tennessee Press, 1996); *The Best in Tent Camping: Southern Appalachian & Smoky Mountains* (Menasha Ridge Press, 1999); *Day & Overnight Hikes in Shenandoah National Park* (Menasha Ridge Press, 1998); *The Best in Tent Camping: West Virginia* (Menasha Ridge Press, 2000); *Day & Overnight Hikes in Monongahela National Forest* (Menasha Ridge Press, 2000); and *The Best in Tent Camping: Florida* (Menasha Ridge Press, 2000). In addition, he has authored numerous magazine articles.

Today, Johnny continues to write about, and travel extensively to, all four corners of the United States indulging in a variety of outdoor pursuits. He has recently completed another book for Menasha Ridge Press, *Mount Rogers Outdoor Recreation Handbook*.